# THE

## *Bristol*

## KSW

There have been few major cities in which the bus fleet contained a high percentage of a very standardised chassis and body combination. Bristol, however, possessed a fleet of nearly 250 essentially similar, open-platformed highbridge KSWs, operated within its bounds by Bristol Joint Services. This accounted for approximately 50 per cent of the otherwise varied BJS fleet. The buses continued to maintain busy routes well into the 1970s, their ruggedness and reliability being greatly appreciated. Caught in the autumn sunshine at Staple Hill Depot, Bristol, in 1972, are No. C8312 (UHY 352) of 1955, and No. C8407 (YHT 903), of 1957 vintage.

*Graham Jones*

THORNBURY
PATCHWAY
ALMONDSBURY
RUDGEWAY
ALVESTON
30

NAE 64
8004

The classic, clean lines of the Eastern Coach Works-bodied Bristol KSW are well captured by this photograph. The big windows, with pleasantly radiused corners, were inset to allow a particularly smooth interior finish. The slender pillars, especially those at the corners, permitted excellent visibility for the passengers, while the gently curved front profile and curves to the baseline of the windscreen and bulkhead windows made the bus easy on the eye. This example, photographed shortly after entering service in 1951, is one of 25 pre-production KSW6Bs, although the features would just as easily apply to a 1957 KSW. The large, single-piece destination box shows it to be one of Bristol Tramways' fleet, in which it was numbered 8004 (NAE 64).

*Michael Mogridge*

# THE

*Bristol*

KSW

# Graham Jones
# &
# Allan Macfarlane

These two pictures illustrate admirably the prime differences between the 7ft. 6in. wide KS model (top) and its 8ft. wide counterpart, the KSW (lower). Apart from the obvious difference in width, the windscreen and dash differed slightly. The beading around the edge of the dash on the KSW curved across the top to a point adjacent to the shoulder of the radiator, whereas on the KS, the beading took a higher course and continued over the radiator. This taller dash resulted in a slightly shallower windscreen. The 7ft. 6in. bodies that were built between 1954 and 1957, for Brighton and York-West Yorkshire, did not strictly comply to this rule, as can be seen elsewhere in this book. The buses acting here as a yardstick are both members of Western National's well kept fleet, and were already approaching 20 years of age when photographed in Bridgwater in March 1969. The KS is No. 1809 (LTA 828) while the KSW is No. 1819 (LTA 838).
*Graham Jones*

# Oxford
# Publishing Co.

ISBN 0-86093-347-4

Typesetting by:
Aquarius Typesetting Services, New Milton, Hants.

Printed in Great Britain by:
Biddles Ltd., Guildford, Surrey.

Published by:
Oxford Publishing Co.
Link House
West Street
POOLE, Dorset

# FOREWORD

Allan and I have devoted a great deal of our attention to the KSW class, ever since its heyday, in the 1950s and 1960s. During 1973, when few KSWs were left in service, we formed The KSW Club (now reconstituted as The Bristol Interest Circle) and produced a bi-monthly KSW newsletter, to keep tracks on the survivors. We now extend our thanks to many friends from The KSW Club, who provided valuable information, to the PSV Circle, whose publications have been very useful reference works, and to the photographers, particularly Bob Mack, who willingly gave permission to reproduce their pictures in this book.

*Graham Jones*
*Poole, Dorset*
*Allan Macfarlane,*
*Bristol*
*September 1984*

# CONTENTS

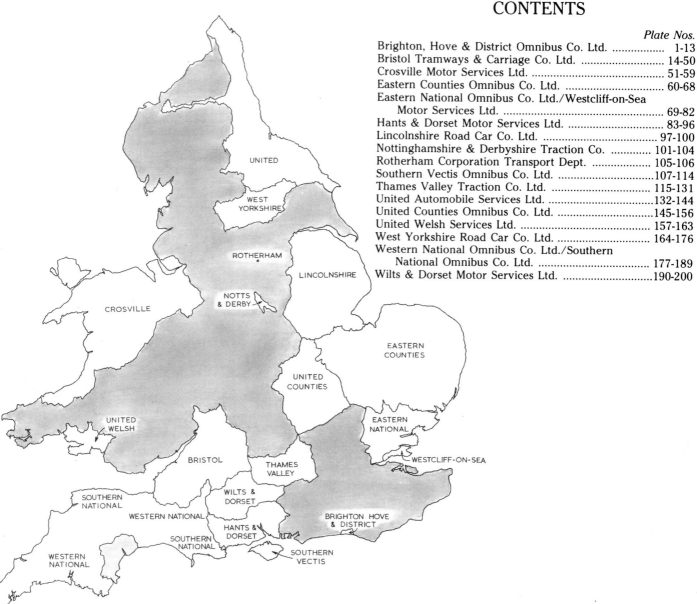

# INTRODUCTION

'What do the letters KSW mean?' That's a question that is often asked! Firstly, K is the designation of the chassis from which the KS/KSW was developed; S stands for 'short', as it was the shorter of two proposed new derivatives (the longer model never entered production); and W means 'wide', the KSW taking advantage of the then newly-permitted, increased maximum width. In the 1950 amendments to the Construction & Use Regulations, which govern the maximum dimension of buses and coaches, double-deckers henceforth could measure 27ft. x 8ft., instead of 26ft. x 7ft. 6in. The Bristol KS and KSW chassis were introduced as a direct result of these amendments.

Bristol Tramways, the builders, as well as increasing the wheelbase of its K family chassis from 16ft. 3in. to 16ft. 8in., also moved the front bulkhead rearwards by 6in., so that the long Gardner 6LW engine could be accommodated, without modifying the standard chassis. The new models were termed KS when built to the 7ft. 6in. width, or KSW when built to the 8ft. maximum. The Eastern Coach Works body for the new chassis was restyled, to produce an extremely elegant product . . . as can be seen throughout these pages!

The new models were introduced in mid-1950, during the maker's 80th sanction; chassis 80.001-053 were K5Gs, K6Bs and K6Gs, and 80.054 onwards were KS5Gs and KS6Bs. Twenty five pre-production KSW6Bs were built for assessment, with chassis Nos. 80.101-125, after which chassis up to 80.200 were further KSs. More KSs were built to the 82nd sanction (82.001-086), before the KSW became standard, except for special orders. The subsequent sanctions were numbers 84, 86, 90, 92, 94, 98, 102, 106 and 118.

The introduction of the revolutionary lowheight Bristol Lodekka, in 1954, soon made the lowbridge bus obsolete! Production of highbridge KSs and KSWs continued, until the series ceased production in 1957. A total of 1,352 KS/KSW chassis had been built.

The engines available were the Gardner 5LW 5 cylinder 7 litre diesel of 85b.h.p., Gardner 6LW 6 cylinder 8.4 litre diesel of 112 b.h.p., and Bristol AVW 6 cylinder 8.1 litre diesel of 100b.h.p. Although the chassis were designed with the 6LW in mind, it was 1952 before 6LWs were installed! The side panel to the bonnet contained two holes, for ease of access to engine components. Their positions varied according to the engine type, the holes for Gardner engines being at the same height as each other, while they were set diagonally for the Bristol engine.

The lower saloon measured 17ft. 5in. in length, which was only one inch longer than that of the K. The capacity of the lower saloon was 28 seats, with 27 seats upstairs in a lowbridge bus, or 32 in the highbridge variant.

Reference is made throughout this book to 'Orders' for a particular year; this indicates the year for which delivery was planned, although it often overlapped into the following year. Buses of the 1950 and 1951 orders were distinguished by the horizontal lower edge to the canopy (see Frontispiece) and London-style seats (see Plate 202); from 1952, the lower edge of the canopy sloped towards the bulkhead (see Plate 26) and higher backed seats were installed (Plate 203). Variations are highlighted throughout the book.

Eastern Coach Works offered highbridge and lowbridge versions of the KS and KSW body. Due to its restricted height, the lowbridge version had a more cramped appearance, but this, if anything, accentuated the length of the side windows. The intrusion of the sunken upper-deck gangway into the offside of the lower saloon, caused the height of the lower-deck windows to be reduced slightly, whereas the cream waistband became deeper. The bus shown is United Automobile No. BBL66 (PHN 828), a 1952 lowbridge KSW6B. Clearly discernible are the inclined, pressed-metal registration plate, surmounted by one brake light and one tail light, and the continuous vertical nearside edge to the platform rear wall; these items were redesigned in 1954, as shown in insert *(right)*, upon the introduction of two tail lights, as required by law. In 1967, this bus was one of four sold by United to Thames Valley, for further service.

*Courtesy ECW*

Brighton, Hove & District Omnibus Co. Ltd. ran an all-urban network of services within these popular Sussex holiday resorts, those in the former town being largely in conjunction with the Corporation Transport, and some of these were also in association with Southdown Motor Services, who were eventually to take control of BH&D.

KSWs figured extensively in the fleet, the total (including KSs) being 82 buses out of 154 vehicles. They were probably the most impressive-looking examples too, wearing a unique livery of red with extensive areas of deep cream, and equipped with enormous destination boxes (a sign of their Thomas Tilling heritage). They also carried running numbers — another London feature — and in this they were somewhat untypical, as not only were individual buses allocated to a particular route, but to a strict duty as well. The operator had no requirements for lowbridge buses (or single deckers), and BH&D was notable, with Bristol Omnibus alone, in ordering K class Bristols right up to the end of production in 1957.

The 1950 order moved into eight-footers right from the word go, and Nos. 6419-26 (FNJ 101-108), although on KS5G chassis, had 8ft. wide H6OR bodywork. Preceding these into service, however, were Nos. 6427-9 (FNJ 109-111), which were three pre-production KSW6Bs.

To the 1951 order, seven more KSW6Bs were built, to become Nos. 6430-6 (GNJ 995-998/991-993). In the summer of 1953, No. 6436 was converted to a KSW6G, rather interestingly. Gardner 6LW engines were also fitted to the 1952 order, after which all further deliveries were thus powered. These 1952 buses were Nos. 6437-46, registered GPM 500-2,900-2, and GPN 991-4

The 1953 batch comprised fifteen KSW6Gs, Nos. 6447-61 (HAP 985-999). It was on members of this batch that experiments with ventilators took place: Nos. 6460/1 were equipped with Beetonson 'Rapide Type W' ventilators (a type that combines slider and hopper principles) alternating with standard ECW sliders.

Another fifteen KSW6Gs were built to the 1954 order, namely Nos. 6462-76 (JAP 500-14). Again Beetonson vents were fitted, although the actual positioning varied slightly on individual vehicles. Also, rain-deflecting louvres, popular in pre-war days, were fitted above all side windows, which gave

a most unusual effect. Both vents and louvres, and the green interior trim which these buses had, became standard from then on, except for the first four 1955 buses, Nos. 6477-80 (KAP 551-4), which had ECW vents and no louvres!

The delivery of these buses coincided with a modification to the fleet numbering system, whereby the Tilling '6' prefix was dropped — indeed Nos. 6478/80 only carried the '6' prefix on the cab front. The other four buses of the order, KNJ 556-9 (note the confusing registrations of this and other batches), first entered service numbered 481-4. By now, incidentally, KSWs were only being built for Brighton and the Bristol group.

Eight more KSW6Gs were delivered in 1956 which, for the first time, had matching fleet and registration numbers; Nos. 485-92 (LNJ 485-92).

The year 1957 was announced as being the final year in which the K class Bristol was to be available, and BH&D caused a sensation in ordering 7ft. 6in. wide KSs! Eight buses with 6LW engines were called for (thus becoming the only KS6Gs in existence) and ECW built 62-seat bodies for them (H34/28R). They were numbered 493-500 (MPM 493-500) and were actually the last 'K's built (chassis 118.038-045).

During 1954/5, some essentially similar bodies, but slightly shorter in the cab section, were built on to six wartime 'K' chassis, two being K5Gs Nos. 6374/5 (CPM 16/7) and the other four being ex-London Transport K6As, now numbered 5996-9 (HGC 247/3/4/54). The former pair had a surprisingly short life, being withdrawn in 1962. Nos. 996-9, as the London buses had become, went in 1965.

Withdrawal of the KS5Gs and KSWs began in 1965, in which year Nos. 426, one of the KS5Gs, became a driver trainer. On 1st January 1969, an early act of the newly-formed National Bus Company was to place BH&D under the control of Southdown Motor Services Ltd. Nos. 450/2-83/5-500 passed to Southdown ownership (together with driver-trainer No. 442, which had replaced No. 426 in 1968), and in the summer, these gained a prefix again, this time a '2'. All remaining KSWs and the KS6Gs were withdrawn by 1972, and it was only a matter of time before Brighton, Hove & District itself passed into history. However, Nos. 2442/77 survived as trainers with Southdown until 1977 — still in BH&D's red and cream livery, although with Southdown fleetnames.

*Plate 1:* Like a stick of rock, this picture has 'Brighton' written all through it! It depicts a red and cream KSW, with an enormous, well-worded destination display, and the vehicle is parked on the right-hand side of the road alongside the Old Steine gardens. No. 430 (GNJ 995) was the first of the 1951 order for KSW6Bs and from this angle, another unusual Brighton feature can be seen, whereby the underside of the canopy was painted silver. The BH&D fleet operated from two depots, at Whitehawk in Brighton, and Conway Street in Hove. Since the late 1950s, allocations were shown by colour coding the running-number plate (on the side, below the first window), whereby black indicated Whitehawk and green, Conway Street. No. 430 has a green plate and was photographed in April 1961, one month before route 14 was renumbered 54.

*Allan Macfarlane*

*Plate 2:* Numerically, the first KS/KSW class buses in the Brighton, Hove & District fleet were the eight KS5G eight-footers, Nos. 6419-26 (later renumbered 419-26). This August 1961 view of No. 424 (FNJ 106) in Western Road, Brighton, clearly shows, by the shadows under the wheel arches, an effect of mounting 8ft. wide bodywork on the narrower KS chassis. The FNJ-registered KSs and KSWs were the only ones in Brighton with the registration plate at the foot of the radiator.

*G. Mead*

*Plate 3:* Brighton's three pre-production KSW6Bs entered service on 1st January 1951, a couple of months ahead of the 8ft. KSs. No. 429 (FNJ 111) displays the revised fleet-name brought in following the introduction of the Brighton Area Transport Services agreement, in 1961, in association with Brighton Corporation and Southdown. The earlier fleetname (*see Plate 1*) had also been carried on the Corporation's buses, which even shared the red and cream livery. No. 429 is shown at Old Steine on route 54, which had formerly been numbered 14 (*see Plate 1 again*). The new linens for route 54, however, carried no intermediate points, heralding a change for the KS/KSW class. As can be seen, the destination box was not masked at this time (*see Plate 6*).

*R. H. G. Simpson*

*Plate 4:* There is plenty of street scenery in this view of 1951 KSW6B No. 6432 (GNJ 997), ranging from the Morris 8 Series E, to trolleybus overhead wires. Route 38 was one of the first to employ KSWs. The blinds show another London practice, whereby there was a white division between displays, to assist with accurate lining up (obviously, not infallible!). Although up to five intermediate points were shown, BH&D still found it necessary to use slipboards on occasion, the brackets for which can be seen below the main indicator.

*Howard Butler*

*Plate 5:* The 1952 batch of KSWs started Brighton's allegiance to the Gardner 6LW engine; the company thus became the only one to employ both 5LW and 6LW engines in its KS/KSW class buses. The sloping canopy and high-backed seats can be seen in this view of No. 441 (GPM 901), photographed in September 1959, when parking was still permitted around the eternally-busy Old Steine. One of this batch of KSW6Gs, No. 6439 (GPM 502), was demonstrated to Notts & Derby in the summer of 1953.

*C. W. Routh*

*Plate 6:* The last two members of Brighton's 1953 batch, HAP 998/9, were experimentally equipped with Beetonson ventilators in the first and third bays of each deck, except for the nearside of the upper deck, where the second and fourth bays carried Beetonsons. The former bus is shown at Brighton Station, when numbered 2460 under Southdown ownership. It clearly demonstrates the rather unattractive masking of the destination box, applied to the whole class from the autumn of 1962. By this time, July 1969, spotlights had been fitted for the first time.

*P. J. Relf*

*Plate 7:* In contrast to the bus seen in *Plate 6*, No. 6476 (JAP 514), the last of the 1954 order, carries Beetonson vents in the first and third nearside bays and second and fourth offside bays. There were, however, many variations within this batch. Also to be seen in this view at Southwick Green are the old-fashioned metal louvres, placed above all the side windows, and the original position for the running number. No slipboard brackets are yet fitted beneath the destination box.

*Howard Butler*

*Plate 8:* The first four buses of the 1955 delivery, KAP 551-4, reverted to ECW sliding vents and carried no louvres. Seen heading for Southwick, No. 480 (KAP 554) swings round the Aquarium roundabout and clearly shows that a standard intermediate/route-number blind was used in the side destination box. In 1962, however, No. 479 was experimentally equipped with three-track route number indicators in the intermediate boxes, but subsequent conversions used large single blinds, as shown in *Plate 6*.

*R. H. G. Simpson*

Plate 9: No. 489 (LNJ 489) of 1956, demonstrates, possibly better than any other, the classic Brighton bus. The metal louvres, the Beeton-son vents, the red and cream livery and large destination indicators were items found on no other company's KSWs. Twenty seven of Brighton's KSWs carried the louvres, incidentally, as did the eight KS6Gs. No. 489 is seen among typical Brighton scenery in Marine Parade, during April 1959.

*G. Mead*

Plate 10: This photograph, taken at Old Steine in July 1970, permits several comparisons to be made. On the left is a 1953 KSW6G, No. 2452 (HAP 990), while on the right is one of the 1957 KS6Gs, No. 2499 (MPM 499). As both widths of bodywork employed the same size glazing, the corner panelling makes the differences between the narrow and wide bodies very apparent. Also seen in this view are the two styles of rear registration plate, back lights and platform openings, the KSW being similar to the bus shown in the photograph in the Introduction, while the KS has a glazed plate and a second tail light 'outrigged' from the foot of the rear wall nearside edge. Both buses are working services that were formerly Brighton Corporation trolleybus routes, these having been transferred to BH&D in May 1963. A common feature used by seaside operators was the honesty fare box — one can be seen on the platform of No. 2499.

*Graham Jones*

*Plate 11:* Quite a surprise was caused when BH&D ordered 7ft. 6in. wide KS6Gs for 1957 delivery. The company had missed taking any in 1950, but some narrow streets in the area evidently swayed the operator's decision. These KSs differed in detail from those built between 1950 and 1952, principally in that the beading on the cab dash was of KSW pattern, even though they had the shallower windscreens. They also had sloping canopies, and so forth. Seating 62, these had the largest capacity of any KS/KSW class buses and were not exceeded in BH&D's fleet until FLFs arrived, nine years later. No. 497 (MPM 497) is joined at Old Steine by No. 442 (GPM 902), the latter being partly obscured by the handle for 'pulling the frog' on the trolleybus overhead wires.

*R. H. G. Simpson*

*Plate 12:* New in 1945, Brighton, Hove & District's Nos. 6374/5 (CPM 16/7) were originally K6As, with Park Royal utility bodies. In 1954, both were re-equipped with Gardner 5LW engines and were rebodied by ECW with new H6OR bodies, of KS pattern. As can be seen in this view of No. 6375, however, the cab section was reduced in length, the leading upper-deck side window being correspondingly shorter. There was, furthermore, no space between the front wing and the bulkhead. The beading on the dash is a blend of KS and KSW patterns, and the windscreen is deeper than on the KS. Compare this view of No. 6375 with *Plate 8*. These two 1954 bodies only saw eight years service in Brighton!

*R. H. G. Simpson*

*Plate 13:* Following the rebodying of Nos. 6374/5, Brighton, Hove & District decided, in 1955, to have new bodies built for their four ex-London Transport K6As, Nos. 5996-9 (HGC 247/3/4/54. The new bodies presented the same appearance as Nos. 6374/5 (*see Plate 12*), and this offside view shows well the shorter window ahead of the driver's door and the arched aperture to the filler cap. These four buses lasted longer with BH&D than did the CPMs, but even ten years was a short life for such fine bodywork. No. 997, once London Transport's No. B18, stands in Western Road, Brighton, in September 1962.

*P. J. Relf*

For the Bristol Tramway & Carriage Company, the KSW proved a particularly suitable bus with which to undertake large-scale fleet renewal during the 1950s. Its 60 seat capacity was most useful and its reliability was much appreciated in Bristol's hilly terrain. The intense network of routes serving the City of Bristol, run in collaboration with Bristol Corporation, was just part of a large territory encompassing other conurbations such as Bath, Gloucester and Cheltenham. This resulted in the company's stock of KS and KSW buses being far and away the largest such fleet in the country, totalling close on 400 units! This was about four times as large as the nearest rival, and was helped by the fact that few low bridges plagued operations, meaning that the Bristol Lodekka played a relatively minor role following its introduction in 1954; the KSW remained a principal choice right up to 1957.

The company's sphere of operations was divided into several subsidiary fleets, although all were integrated to a greater or lesser extent. Buses owned by Bristol Tramways to work the length and breadth of their territory formed the 'Country Services' fleet. In Bristol, a fleet was managed by Bristol Joint Services and was known as the 'City' fleet (fleet numbers were distinguished by a 'C' prefix). The Bristol coat of arms adorned the side panels, in place of a fleetname, on both 'City' and 'Country' buses. BT&CC also managed services in Gloucester on behalf of Gloucester Corporation, the buses here bearing the Gloucester coat of arms. Two subsidiary companies worked from Bath, namely Bath Electric Tramways Ltd. and Bath Tramways Motor Co. Ltd. The buses of both fleets carried a fleetname of Bath Services. The most recently acquired subsidiary, transferred from Red & White Services to Bristol Tramways' control by the BTC in 1950, was Cheltenham District Traction Company. Happily, Bristol Tramways retained Cheltenham District's dignified dark red livery, with cream window surrounds, for additional stock. The numbering system in two figures was also continued. On the company's other buses, Tilling green livery was carried. However, the standard Tilling destination boxes were never specified, the company preferring single-piece boxes measuring, initially, 36in. x 18in. Before 1951, each fleet had its own series of fleet numbers.

Twenty two KS6Bs were delivered to the 'City' fleet in 1950/1, numbered C3456-77 (NAE 11-32). They had high-bridge bodies, as did all but a small minority of the company's double deckers. At the end of 1950, the first KS6B for 'Country Services' arrived, numbered 3784 (NAE 33). On 1st January 1951, however, this bus was transferred to the Gloucester city fleet and renumbered 1520, being joined at the same time by Nos. 1521-6 (NAE 34-9).

Also on 1st January, the first KSWs entered service, on trunk 'Country' routes. Not only were these eight-footers distinguished by white steering wheels, but by a completely new numbering series, 8000 onwards! This initial batch of eight pre-production KSW6Bs was numbered 8000-7 (NAE 60-67), the first three being the first KSWs constructed. Following on were eighteen 8ft. wide KS6Bs, which were numbered 8008-25 (NAE 40-57), after which came Nos. 8026/7 (NAE 58/9), KSW6Bs. Nos. 8015-20 were Bath Services buses.

The next batch of buses was composed entirely of KSW6B chassis. Some of the first to arrive were the first Bristols for Cheltenham District. Registered NHY 938/9, their fleet numbers were 80 and 81. It was a coincidence that the first eight-footers in Cheltenham should also have fleet numbers beginning with 8. The first-named was a particularly interesting bus, as it carried lowbridge bodywork, for town route 12. In later years, a prefix 'L' was added. Bath Services took delivery of Nos. 8028-34 (NHY 950-6), but the remaining 43 of this batch were all destined for the 'City' fleet! They were

numbered C8035-77 (NHY 957-999). It will be noted that all divisions, except CDTC, now shared a common numbering series. An unusual feature of this 1951 order was that, although low-backed seats were installed, the frames on the gangway side were vertical, rather than tapered.

The taller seats and sloping canopies were a feature of the 1952 order, which was the most varied series to be delivered to BT&CC. The first to arrive were 'Country' buses Nos. 8078-81 (OHY 941-4), but these were novel in having enclosed platforms and saloon heaters. 'City' buses Nos. C8082-5 (OHY 956-9) followed them. The next ten buses were the most interesting of the order — not only did they have platform doors and heaters, but they were of lowbridge layout. Numbered L8086-95, they were registered OHY 937/4/6/8/9/1/5/2/3/40! Further interest was generated by Nos. L8087/91/3-5, as these were the company's first Gardner-powered KSW6Gs. These ten lowbridge KSWs were shared between BT&CC and Bath Services, the latter receiving Nos. L8086/8-90/5. No more lowbridge KSWs were to be delivered to the firm.

Bath also operated the next highbridge KSWs, Nos. 8096-8102 (OHY 945-51), of which Nos. 8098/9 were KSW6Gs. Although open-backed, heaters were installed. Cheltenham District received Nos. 82-85 (OHY 952-5) at about the same time.

The balance of the order was delivered to the 'City' and Gardner 6LW engines were featured in many. The batch was No. C8103-32 (OHY 960-89), the KSW6Gs being Nos. C8103-6/15-7/24-32. The next fleet number was carried not by a KSW, but a Lodekka. No. L8133 was the first pre-production LD6B and was taken for assessment.

By contrast to that of 1952, the 1953 KSW order lacked variety, as all but two ran for Bristol Joint Services and all but one were KSW6Bs. The batch comprised Nos. C8134-71 (PHW 959-88/90/2-8), of which No. C8166 was the sole KSW6G. The two that went elsewhere were Cheltenham's No. 86 and 87 (PHW 989/91).

For 1954, BT&CC signed the largest single order ever placed for KSWs! No fewer than seventy one buses were called for, but the batch was quite uncomplicated. Cheltenham District received No. 88 (SHW 341), their first Bristol with green interior trim. Then, concurrently, 'Country' and 'City' routes were furnished with Nos. 8172-99 (SHW 342-69), enclosed-platform KSW6Gs, and Nos. C8200-41 (SHW 370-411), which were KSW6Bs, except for Gardner-engined Nos. C8200/1. Nos. 8172-4 were Bath Services stock. Following a change in the law, two rear lights appeared on Nos. 8187 and C8205, the rear registration plates henceforth being behind glass windows and a flush panel replacing the recessed lower-deck offside quarter-bay.

Delivery of these 71 KSWs was followed by the company's first batch of Lodekkas, Nos. L8242-62 and CDTC No. 89. The 1955 programme featured many more LDs, but KSWs still dominated. Bath Services received Nos. 8265-70 (UHY 376-81), more H6ORD-bodied KSW6Gs, while Bristol's 'Country' fleet took similar buses, Nos. 8334-49 (UHY 382-97). The 'City' fleet's quota was Nos. C8301-33 (UHY 341-73), all KSW6Bs. The two Cheltenham buses, Nos. 90 and 91 (UHY 374/5) were the first KSW6Gs for that division.

These UHYs introduced a shallower destination indicator to the fleet, with a depth of 12in.

Thirty two KSWs were ordered for 1956, all but two being for 'City' routes. The first ten, Nos. C8350-9, used the last of the 99 registrations booked for 1955 deliveries, in being UHY 430-9. Ten identical KSW6Bs followed, numbered C8360-9 (WHW 801-10), while Nos. C8370-9 (WHW 811-20) were KSW6Gs. Cheltenham District's Nos. 92 and 93

(WHW 821/2) were also KSW6Gs and were their last new KSWs.

The year 1957 was announced as being the last year in which the K class Bristol would be available; indeed only Bristol and Brighton, Hove & District were still taking the model. Bristol's final order was destined for the 'City' entirely. It was composed of KSW6Bs Nos. C8405-23 (YHT 901-19) and KSW6Gs Nos. C8424-31 (YHT 920-7). As Brighton ordered KSs for 1957, these turned out to be the last KSWs built. BT&CC's intake had comprised twenty nine 7ft. 6in. KSs, eighteen 8ft. KSs, eleven lowbridge KSWs, and 338 highbridge KSWs, totalling 396 units!

Another event of 1957 was that the company's title was changed, to Bristol Omnibus Company Ltd. An interesting experiment involved No. C8234 in 1959. The bus received an illuminated offside advertisement panel, but as tungsten bulbs were used, the results were not very successful and the equipment was removed during 1960.

Inter-fleet transfers took place on occasions, involving a small number of KSWs . . . and one KS worthy of note; In 1968, the last KS in the fleet, Gloucester's No. G1526, was surprisingly transferred to 'Country Services', losing its 'G' prefix, and worked out its last summer at Weston-super-Mare. Two KSWs were acquired, on 1st January 1970, with the services and stock of Western National's Wiltshire area.

Withdrawals began in 1965 and progressed until, by 1973, the only survivors were eighteen 'City' KSW6Gs and two similar buses with Cheltenham District. No withdrawals then occurred for a year, but from late 1974, a steady trickle of buses was laid aside. This continued until the spring of 1976, when just two 'City' buses remained active. The final pair was No. C8374 (WHW 815), still wearing Tilling green livery, and leaf green No. C8428 (YHT 924). Both KSWs participated in a 'Farewell Tour', arranged by the authors of this book, in May 1976, and by the end of the month, these, the last standard KSWs remaining in public service in the country, were withdrawn.

*Plate 14:* Just a quick glance at this bus will be sufficient to tell that it belongs to Bristol Tramways. The large, single piece destination box was a feature of post-war deliveries and the printing of the linens was commendably clear. No. C3475 (NAE 30) was one of 22 KS6Bs placed in the 'City' fleet, under the control of Bristol Joint Services, during 1950/1. The high position of the registration plate on the KS enabled the company to continue placing fleet numbers on the dash. The photograph was taken at Sea Mills Square, the bus having just arrived on service 1C, passing the birthplace of the chassis en route, in Brislington.

*Michael Mogridge*

*Plate 15:* In November 1965, by which time there were only about a dozen Ks left in the 'City' fleet, bus service frequencies in Bristol underwent considerable retrenchment. The resultant fleet reductions saw the end of service for the remaining Ks and all the KSs. However, the opportunity was taken of updating the driver training fleet with some of these KSs. Five buses were modified with cut-away bulkheads, a raised instructor's seat, etc., and were repainted with an orange band below the lower-deck windows, emerging as Nos. W114-8 (NAE 28/3, 30-2) formerly Nos. C3474/68/75-7. They spent six or seven years training drivers in Bristol, but did not last long enough to be considered for repainting in the later cream trainer livery. No. W115 is seen here at Muller Road Depot, in December 1968. Amid the line of KSWs beyond is No. C8431 (YHT 927), the last KSW to have been built.

*Graham Jones*

*Plate 16:* A very large proportion of Bristol Omnibus Company's 1951-57 buses were fitted with this distinctive, if unattractive, pattern of T-shaped destination box from 1960. The top site maintained the 36in. width of the earlier box, and was combined with a four-track numeral box ('City' buses carried route numbers only at the rear). Whilst the majority of KSWs were equipped with this indicator, the only 'City' KSs to receive it were Nos. C3459/60/4/5/7/77. No. C3459 (NAE 14) is seen here outside Lewis' store in The Haymarket on 13th May 1961, and the style of 'T' box and the height of the registration plate somehow accentuate the vehicle's 7ft. 6in. width. The pressed aluminium fleet number plates and flashing trafficators were also introduced in 1960.

*Allan Macfarlane*

*Plate 17:* Buses allocated to the Gloucester city fleet displayed the Gloucester coat of arms on the side panels, and originally had their own series of fleet numbers. A 'G' prefix was added to these numbers in 1959, as illustrated here by No. G1521 (NAE 34), a 1950-built KS6B. The side fleet number plates are set back to enable flashing trafficators to be fitted later. From 1955, new buses were delivered with shallower destination boxes, reduced from 18in. to 12in., and subsequently, many earlier buses had aluminium masks, with rubber-mounted 12in. apertures, placed over their 18in. sites, as shown here, and in *Plate 15.*

*Geoff Stainthorpe*

*Plate 18:* No. G1525 (NAE 38) had quite an eventful life. Firstly, it was the only KS/KSW class bus to be repainted in Bristol's brighter livery of 1950/1, with much more cream, then in 1954, it nearly came to grief in a terrifying collision with a train at the Barton Street level crossing in Gloucester. The cab and first two offside bays were extensively damaged, but the bus was repaired with little sign that anything had been wrong . . . other than on the dash, where straight beading was applied, instead of the usual curved strip. Next, in 1959, No. G1525 became one of only three buses, other than Bristol 'City' KSWs, to receive the company's initial pattern of T-type destination box conversion, featuring a single route number track (*see also Plate 24*). It is in this condition that No. G1525 was pictured, passing No. G1522 while working route 3. Nos. G1520-6 were all eventually to receive four-track 'T' boxes.

*R. F. Mack*

*Plate 19:* Several of Bristol Omnibus Company's early eight-footers became associated with Weston-super-Mare town services, through to the mid-1960s. In April 1963, No. 8010 (NAE 42), an 8ft. KS6B, was photographed leaving the Grand Pier on cross-town route 40. The destination box shows a later and more economical way of reducing the site to accommodate 12in. displays (*see Plate 17*) although a 4-track 'T' box was soon to be fitted. The bus still has the unglazed quarter panel alongside the platform, but even this late in its life, this panel was to become glazed. Indeed, the only examples to retain the panel until withdrawal were Nos. C3469, G8012, 8019, C8035/40! Note the fleetname 'BRISTOL', which replaced the Bristol coat of arms from 1961.

*P. J. Relf*

*Plate 20:* Bath Services operated 8ft. KSs Nos. 8015-20 (NAE 47-52). The fleetname was common to buses owned by both Bath Electric Tramways Ltd. and Bath Tramways Motor Co. Ltd. Similarly, services were licensed to one company or the other, the former being responsible for many of Bath city's busy double-deck routes. There were, however, no restrictions on the use of the buses of either firm. No. 8015, a BET-owned bus, is seen in London Road, passing the Bath Depot. The simplified destination display was, unfortunately, widely used in Bath during the 1960s.

*Graham Jones Collection*

*Plate 21:* When new, the first eight-footers in the Bristol Tramways fleet were employed on trunk 'Country' routes, as exemplified by No. 8021 (NAE 53), a KS6B, seen here in Bristol (when traffic ran anti-clockwise round one island on the Centre) prior to starting the long trip to Swindon. The shadows under the wheel arches highlight the effect of 8ft. bodywork on the 7ft. 6in. chassis. In January 1956, No. 8021 was transferred to the Gloucester city fleet to become one of that section's first eight-footers. This followed three months of trial with sister vehicle No. 8025, which was renumbered in a new series, as No. 1800, the success of which led to KSW No. 8001 and KSs Nos. 8011/12/21 becoming Nos. 1801-4. In 1966, these buses reverted to their original numbers, but retained the 'G' prefix gained in 1959.

*S. N. J. White*

*Plate 22:* Seven of the earliest members of the 1951 KSW6B order were allocated to Bath Services. Bath Electric Tramways' No. 8032 (NHY 954) was one of the longest-lived of the NHYs, and is seen here at Parade Gardens in February 1968, during its last few months of service. It was one of several early machines to retain its single-piece destination boxes until withdrawal, albeit heavily masked to an 8in. display. The Bath area routes had been renumbered into the upper 100s and 200s in September 1967. It will be noted that following the adoption of a square registration plate, fleet numbers could no longer be applied to the front of KSWs.

*Dave Withers*

*Plate 23:* A splendid example of a Bristol Tramways KSW at its best, when brand-new and with fully utilised 18in. destination box, is No. C8036 (NHY 958), the second KSW delivered to the 'City' fleet, in Janaury 1952. It stands at the Carey's Lane terminus at Old Market, a scene that has long disappeared in favour of the inner ring road. Some of these NHYs were affected by the 1965 service reductions (*see Plate 15*), and eight were transferred to the 'Country' or Bath Services fleets, henceforth being numbered 8038-40 and 8051-5. The remaining 'City' examples were withdrawn by early 1967, but later, seven were reinstated with Bath Services (now numbered 8070-5) or the 'Country' fleet (No. 8077), principally to release FSF Lodekkas for sale to Western National. These seven only survived for a further year or so.

*S. N. J. White*

*Plate 24:* Following the introduction of T-type destination boxes on new Lodekkas in 1958, Bristol Omnibus Company soon started fitting 'City' KSWs with 'T' boxes, although these featured a small, single track route number site, as shown here. The conversions took place quickly and affected very many of the NHY and OHY batches, together with some of the PHW and SHW groups. The only other buses treated were KS No. G1525 (*see Plate 18*), 'Country' KSW No. 8337, and K-type No. 3780. This pattern was short-lived, being superseded by a four-track version (*see Plate 16*), and all the single-track boxes had disappeared by 1964. This July 1960 view shows No. C8074 (NHY 996) at the St. James' Barton roundabout at the top of the Haymarket, with two similarly-equipped KSWs visible beyond, in Marlborough Street, outside the bus station.

*Geoff Stainthorpe*

*Plate 25:* Numerically the first Bristol added to the Cheltenham District fleet was KSW6B No. 80 (NHY 938). This bus differed from all other NHYs in bearing lowbridge bodywork, as it was used for Cheltenham town route 12, which encountered a low bridge in Hatherley Road. No. 80 subsequently gained a prefix 'L' for lowbridge, and also found its way on to other routes on occasions; indeed, it is seen in this picture on route 2, a service associated with CDTC's Guy Arab IIIs for many years. In May 1966, by which time few non-Bristols were left in the BOC fleet, CDTC's Bristols were renumbered into the main series, No. L80 becoming No. L8551. It was withdrawn in 1967.

*R. H. G. Simpson*

*Plate 26:* The 1952 KSW order, the OHYs, was the most varied delivered to Bristol Tramways. Among the 59 buses were ten lowbridge examples, fitted with platform doors and saloon heaters, for 'Country' routes. Five were allocated to Bath Tramways Motor Company and were a familiar sight on service 46 to Chippenham and the lengthy service 50 to Salisbury. No. L8088 (OHY 936) stands at Grand Parade, Bath, when new, accompanied by a lowbridge K, a highbridge KSW and a pre-war L. Bath Services received a sixth lowbridge KSW in 1959, when No. L8094 was transferred from 'Country Services'.

*Michael Mogridge*

*Plate 27:* Stroud Depot was particularly associated with lowbridge K-types, especially those taken over with Western National's operations in 1950, yet only twice has a lowbridge KSW been on its allocation, neither bus remaining particularly long. In February 1966, only nine months before the final lowbridge K was withdrawn from Stroud, No. L8093 (OHY 932) was transferred from Wells, to spend its remaining days at Stroud. It is seen at the bus station, bearing the scroll fleet-name introduced in 1965, and dual-coloured fleet number plates to indicate the allocation. This bus became the last lowbridge double decker in the Bristol fleet, and was withdrawn in July 1968.

*Dave Withers*

*Plate 28:* Bristol Omnibus Company found that the lowbridge KSWs made ideal driver trainers, due to their less-restricted sphere of operation. Even though a section of the sunken gangway had to be removed to permit the installation of the raised instructor's seat, no fewer than seven of the ten lowbridge OHYs were converted to trainers, many replacing early post-war lowbridge Ks. The seven were formerly Nos. L8087/9-91/3-5, which became Nos. W130/27/2/6/8/4/3, respectively, between 1967 and 1969, the first-named being converted two years after its withdrawal from passenger service! In 1971, the seven received the new trainer livery of cream, with orange band, wings and radiator, as shown here on No. W123 (OHY 940), practising hill starts at Stroud Depot. Eventually, this bus became the last of these seven to be withdrawn, in 1977, and it set a company record, having been a trainer for ten years! Highbridge KSWs became trainers, too, principally in Bristol. These were converted from Nos. C8129-31/48, 8192, 8336 and C8407, becoming Nos. W133/4/1/2/5/43/50, respectively.

*Allan Macfarlane*

*Plate 29:* Nos. 8096-8102 (OHY 945-51) were allocated to Bath Tramways Motor Company for use on country routes and, although equipped with five speed gearboxes and saloon heaters, they were not provided with platform doors. Eventually, however, they settled down on Bath city routes, as shown here by No. 8096 in Bloomfield Road, with a 'lazy' destination blind in its panelled-down 12in. box.

*Graham Jones Collection*

*Plate 30:* The application of the attractive Cheltenham District dark red and cream livery is illustrated here by No. 85 (OHY 955). Until about 1965, CDTC had a policy of allocating individual buses to a particular route, so No. 85 was a regular on service 5, between Hester's Way and Lynworth. This panelled 12in. destination box was further masked to 5in. in later years, but it was never converted to the T-type. In the May 1966 renumbering, No. 85 became No. 8556.

*R. F. Mack*

*Plate 31:* The luxury of enclosed platforms and saloon heaters first appeared on Bristol Tramways' buses in 1952, but only on those allocated to 'Country' routes — KSWs built for urban work never even had heaters, if the seven shown in *Plate 29* are excluded. With the narrower entrance, an emergency door had to be provided in the rear wall, as shown here on the third member of the initial batch of these buses, No. 8080 (OHY 943). It is seen in Anchor Road, Bristol, bound for Cheltenham, via Gloucester — such long distance stopping services are now a thing of the past. Nos. 8078-81 were KSW6Bs, but all future enclosed platform highbridge KSWs for Bristol were powered by Gardner 6LW engines.

*Michael Mogridge*

*Plate 33:* There is a railway bridge across St. Luke's Road, Bedminster, Bristol, that is of such a height that should a highbridge bus inadvertently be taken under it, then the roof would be neatly shaved off . . . without one pane of glass even being cracked! Regrettably, between 1965 and 1971, no fewer than six KSWs took this literal 'short cut' when returning to their depot, to avoid heavy traffic on Wells Road. Each bus was from a different batch, but all were too old to be worthy of repair. A further use was found, however, for the second victim, No. C8108 (OHY 965), which was rebuilt to a tree lopper and renumbered W120, in 1967. For many years based on Bath Depot, it initially carried Tilling green livery, as shown by this January 1970 view at Terrace Walk, Bath. Subsequently, it was repainted orange and, most recently, it has emerged in yellow. In September 1983, it passed to the new Cheltenham & Gloucester Omnibus Company, on the formation of this firm to assume responsibility of BOC's northern district, and No. W120 is now based on Stroud. Another low bridge victim to remain in the current fleet is No. C8318 (UHY 358), which, also rebuilt to open-top, has been the carol singer's Christmas fund-raising bus, No. W138, since 1970.

*Dave Withers*

*Plate 32:* In contrast to the 'Country' fleet, Gardner-engined KSWs were very much in the minority in Bristol's 'City' fleet. One of their KSW6Gs, No. C8128 (OHY 985) is seen late in life in June 1968, at the Cheltenham Road terminus of the circuitous 83 service. Horsefair is only one mile away, yet it took an hour to get there! The conductor displays the style of uniform which, although much more businesslike than the NBC uniforms of today, looks rather dated now.

*Graham Jones*

*Plate 34:* All PHW-registered KSWs, apart from two Cheltenham District examples, were Bristol 'City' buses. No. C8136 (PHW 961), one of the first of these 1953 vehicles, is seen in Queen Square, Bristol, in the snow of February 1969 — slush and road salt have left their inevitable mark on the side of the bus. In 1960, by way of assessment, No. C8136 and No. 8032 were fitted with glass fibre panelling below lower-deck window level.

*Graham Jones*

*Plate 35:* Normally, KSWs for each section of the Bristol fleet, within particular registration batches, were grouped together. The exception was the pair of PHW-registered KSW6Bs for Cheltenham District, which were mixed randomly among 'City' vehicles, resulting in CDTC receiving PHW 989 and PHW 991. They were the last Cheltenham KSWs to have red interior trim to complement their dark red exteriors. No. 86 (PHW 989) had been renumbered 8557 by the time it was photographed in The Promenade, in March 1969. Furthermore, wings, wheels and radiators had been repainted deep red instead of black, and bus services in the area had been renumbered into the 500s.

*Graham Jones*

*Plate 36:* The first large batch of enclosed platform KSWs was the SHW series, the first three of which were allocated to Bath Tramways Motor Company in 1954. The middle bus of the trio, No. 8173 (SHW 343) was photographed in the depot yard in June 1964. In 1967, Nos. 8172-4 were joined by no fewer than twelve others of this batch, namely Nos. 8185/7/90-99. All were principally used on Bath city routes and replaced a variety of earlier Bath KSWs and 8ft. KSs. However, withdrawal of the enclosed platform SHWs began in 1968, after only fourteen years of service.

*Geoff Stainthorpe*

*Plate 37:* The first buses with enclosed rear platforms to be allocated to the Gloucester city fleet arrived in December 1965, when Nos. 8182-4 (SHW 352-4) were transferred from the 'Country' fleet. They simply received a 'G' prefix to their numbers, rather than joining the 1800s. In 1967, the local fleet received a 'GLOUCESTER' fleetname beneath the city's coat of arms, as No. G8184 illustrates. The bus is seen in King's Square on a route that traditionally seemed to employ the oldest buses (previously route 3). This popular photographic location was subsequently rebuilt out of all recognition, and pedestrianised.
*Michael Bennett*

*Plate 38:* A small fleet of 'Country' buses was based in Bristol for use on 'City' routes, due to mileage balancing reasons with Bristol Joint Services. These had traditionally been some of the oldest 'Country' double deckers, 8ft. KSs and KSWs not being involved until 1963. The open-platform NAEs were ideally suited, but the KSWs with platform doors were officially stated to be less suitable. Consequently, during 1966/7, the five H6ORD-bodied KSWs then in use on 'City' work, namely Nos. 8078/80 (OHY 941/3), 8179/80 (SHW 349/50) and 8338 (UHY 386) were, most unusually, rebuilt with open platforms! All received the vertical nearside edge to the rear wall, as exemplified by No. 8180. However, in the case of No. 8338, with its glazed rear registration plate, this of course looked a little odd. No further conversions were made, as open-back LDs were moved in from Weston town, and later, enclosed platform buses were accepted. Ironically, these KSWs did not last long in their open-platform state, being withdrawn between 1968 and 1970.
*Dave Withers*

*Plate 39:* Bristol's SHW batch of KSWs, ordered for 1954, was the largest single order ever placed for KSWs, amounting to 71 buses. Two of the 'City' fleet's stock of 41 examples are seen here at the Clyde Road, Redland, terminus of service 14 (developed from the 144 — *see Plate 23),* where No. C8217 (SHW 387) pulls away from No. C8207, in February 1970. From early 1967, 'City' vehicles were given a small Bristol coat of arms above the scroll fleetnames, thereby differing from the 'Country' fleetname for the first time. Introduced six months earlier was the painting of wings, wheels and radiator in Brunswick green, instead of black. All these features are discernible on No. C8217.
*Graham Jones*

*Plate 40:* By early 1973, Cheltenham District's stock of KSWs had diminished to just four KSW6Gs — their two UHYs and two WHWs. All were scheduled to be replaced by their first four Leyland Nationals but, due to the problems affecting the supply of both spares and new vehicles, two KSWs were chosen to be retained in traffic. It was the UHY pair of 1955 (Nos. 8561/2) that had this honour and, in September 1973, both were repainted in the NBC's then new poppy red livery, with Cheltenham fleetnames and the enlarged borough coat of arms. During 1974, fleet number plates were affixed to the front of the Bristol company's buses, instead of the sides, the KSWs then in service being the first since the NAEs to have front-mounted numbers. An unnecessary change to the Cheltenham pair, however, was to move the registration plate towards the radiator, to accommodate the plate and depot code. No. 8561 (UHY 374) is seen at Southam Village during its last week of service, in March 1975. It was the last bus in the company's fleet to retain its original 36in. x 12in. destination boxes until withdrawal. Sister bus No. 8562 was withdrawn on its twentieth 'birthday', 1st October 1975, and in so doing, became the only Bristol group KS/KSW bus to achieve 20 years of passenger service *(but see Plate 36).*

*Graham Jones*

*Plate 41:* Out of the 1955 order for enclosed-platform KSW6Gs, Bath Services received six buses, which were numbered in their own 'group', as 8265-70. No. 8266 (UHY 377) stands at Bath bus station in the mid-1960s, when buses reversed on to the platform. The two Bath firms ceased trading on 1st December 1969, in favour of the Bristol Omnibus Company and, at the time, only ten KSWs remained in Bath ownership (Nos. 8191/3, 8265-70 and 8340/8). A token number of buses retained the Bath Services fleetname, however, including No. 8266. This bus was withdrawn early in 1971, but returned to traffic for the 1971 summer season at Weston-super-Mare, albeit with Bristol fleetnames.

*Graham Jones Collection*

*Plate 42:* Muller Road Depot, in Bristol, had a strong association with the KSW family throughout the life of the class. Even in the late 1960s, some 40 to 50 members were housed here, accounting for a high proportion of the depot's total allocation. It was fitting, therefore, that the last KSWs of all should operate from Muller Road, in 1976. In earlier days, an impressive daytime line-up of KSWs, on lay-over from peak hour services, could be seen on the depot forecourt, as visible in this view of No. C8323 (UHY 363), passing the depot on 12th December 1968, just before service 83 (*see Plate 32*) was converted to one man single-deck operation.

*Graham Jones*

*Plate 43:* Bristol Omnibus Company's 'Country' KSWs of the UHY batch were originally scattered throughout their territory, although by 1970, many had accumulated at Bristol 'City' depots. However, a few remained based at the tiny Highbridge Depot until 1971, to operate the company's last regular rural KSW route, that between Burnham-on-Sea and the company's southernmost outpost, at Bridgwater, where the KSWs met their Western National cousins (*see Plate 186*). No. 8342 (UHY 390) is seen arriving at Bridgwater bus station in March 1969.

*Graham Jones*

*Plate 44:* The number of KSWs remaining in service dropped below 100 during 1971, but the model remained standard stock for several Bristol 'City' routes. One of the busiest, and one that became synonymous with KSWs, was cross-city route 3, a service that received a greatly increased peak hour allocation, to serve the aircraft factories at Filton and Patchway. In this view, in September 1972, No. C8359 (UHY 439) leaves the Filton Church terminus, at the moment that No. C8357 arrives from Whitchurch. These two buses were subsequently to number amongst the last KSW6Bs remaining in Bristol's services, being withdrawn in the autumn of 1973.

*Graham Jones*

*Plate 45:* The 1955 UHY-registered buses had been the first new vehicles to employ a reduced destination screen, measuring 36in. x 12in. (*see Plate 23*). This pattern continued to be specified only for the 1956 and 1957 orders, and is exemplified here by No. C8376 (WHW 817), one of ten KSW6Gs delivered to the 'City' in 1956. The photograph was taken at the St. James' Barton roundabout in July 1960. The similar vintage KSW beyond is carrying a very familiar advertisement of the period. The background to this scene, nowadays, is the amazing Avon House North, which spans North Street, from which the KSW has emerged.

*Geoff Stainthorpe*

*Plate 46:* This low-angle view of 1957 KSW6G No. C8429 (YHT 925) seems to emphasise the ruggedness which earned the model a great reputation. The reliability of the KSW6Gs remaining in service from 1972, Nos. C8370-9 (WHW 811-20) and Nos. C8424-31 (YHT 920-7), was particularly appreciated when the supply of spares, and of new buses, was severely affected in the wake of industrial unrest which hit the country at that time (*see also Plate 40*). Consequently, the withdrawal of the class slowed to a trickle and was not completed until May 1976. No. C8429 itself last ran in service in March 1976 and it was captured in this view in Staple Hill Depot's yard, in September 1972.

*Graham Jones*

*Plate 47:* The last two KSWs to be built, in 1957, are seen together at Staple Hill Depot on 29th April 1973. No. C8431 (YHT 927) retains its Tilling green livery, while No. C8430 (YHT 926) has become one of the first Bristol Omnibus Company vehicles to receive NBC leaf green livery, in January 1973. The smaller fleet number plates, as carried on this bus, had been introduced in 1967, but No. C8431 carries one of the older style . . . in practice, removed from the platform, as the small plate had been lost. The dual-colour code indicates the allocation (on these two buses, green and red for Lawrence Hill and Hanham depots, green and black for Muller Road and Staple Hill). It will be seen that No. C8430 is one of several eight-footers that received black steering wheels from the 1960s.

*Graham Jones*

*Plate 48:* An interesting occurrence of 1st January 1970 was the absorption of Western National's Wiltshire area operations, based on Trowbridge, together with the buses. The varied stock included two 1951 order lowbridge KSW6Bs, LTA 843/4. Bristol numbered them L4155/6 (in a series for 7ft. 6in. lowbridge buses!), but they only saw a few months of public service with BOC. No. L4156 (LTA 844) is seen at the Stratford-upon-Avon bus rally on 31st May 1970, one month before its withdrawal from Trowbridge, and displays the rather oddly-positioned fleetname. Subsequently, both buses were converted to driver trainers (including re-painting into cream — *see Plate 28*), being renumbered W139 and W137, respectively, and in fact, LTA 843 outlived Bristol's own lowbridge trainers, being withdrawn in May 1978.

*Allan Macfarlane*

*Plate 49:* The Bristol Omnibus Company's desire to keep the last eighteen KSW6Gs active as long as practicable, during the hard times of the early 1970s (*see Plate 46*), indirectly resulted in four examples being repainted in the NBC's leaf green livery, during 1973/4 (Nos. C8378, C8424/8/30). Together with Cheltenham District's Nos. 8561/2 (*see Plate 40*), these were the only closed-top KSWs in the country to receive NBC livery. The unique pattern of fleet-name carried by Bristol Joint Services buses at this time is seen in this view of No. C8428 (YHT 924). Also visible are the new front-mounted fleet number plates and depot codes: the letters MR stand for Muller Road, although here, No. C8428 is seen during its most unexpected loan to Winterstoke Road, for the first twelve days of April 1976. Winterstoke Road had not housed KSWs for five years, but maybe wanted a final fling while two examples were still operational. No. C8428 is pictured here turning out of Colston Street on to The Centre, on 8th April. By the end of May, both survivors were withdrawn, No. C8428 on 24th May and, finally, No. C8374 (WHW 815) on Saturday, 29th May 1976 . . . the final KSW in regular NBC public service!

*Graham Jones*

*Plate 50:* Two of the most interesting disposals of Bristol Omnibus Company KSWs concerned Nos. C8426/31 (YHT 922/7), which were exported in 1976 to the district of Macau, near Hong Kong. The buses were operated alongside some Bristol LD and LS models and several elderly Bristol L-types, by Compantia de Autocarros Fok-Lei Limitada (Macau was formerly Portuguese) and wore an attractive yellow and cream livery. Both KSWs were converted to a dual-doorway layout, with an enclosed rear platform and seated conductor, No. C8426 also being rebuilt to open-top. Full depth sliding windows were installed, but note the neat extra half window towards the rear of the upper deck, and the installation of an ECW slider in the platform window. The former No. C8431, the last KSW to have been built, and now registered M-07-16, is seen at its new home during 1977.

*Dave Withers*

With the exception of the huge, 400-strong fleet of Bristol Omnibus Co. KSW class buses, Crosville's fleet was the largest of all, with a total of 112 machines. Yet delivery was concentrated into just three batches, and there was little variety within the fleet. The impressive total was achieved simply because of the sheer quantity of buses that Crosville required to put into service.

After placing some 167 K-type double deckers in service from 1945, together with a number of Leyland Titans, Crosville took a break and ordered no new buses against the 1950 order. Consequently, the company never took any KSs. Deliveries were resumed in 1951 with the appearance, firstly, of ten lowbridge KSW6Bs, Nos. MW418-27 (NFM 50-9). The other fifteen buses of this batch were, interestingly, highbridge vehicles, and were the first highbridge buses ordered by Crosville (note that Crosville, Hants & Dorset, and United each 'introduced' highbridge buses — excluding any second-hand or diverted examples — with their KS or KSW deliveries). The first such bus was a lone KSW5G, the only Gardner-engined KSW to enter the Crosville fleet. It was numbered MG428 (NFM 60), and was followed by KSW6Bs with similar H6OR bodies, Nos. MW429-42 (NFM 61-74).

In the Crosville fleet number prefix system, incidentally, 'M' was the code letter for all oil-engined double deckers, while the second letter was an engine code — 'W' for Bristol engines, 'G' for Gardner.

For 1952, Crosville ordered no fewer than sixty five KSWs, one of the largest single orders ever placed. All were to be lowbridge KSW6Bs. Registered OFM 601-65, they were numbered MW443-499 and MW631-8.

The 1953 KSW order was somewhat smaller, twenty two machines, but the company, at the same time, ordered 58 Lodekkas and subsequently built up a large fleet of over 350 LDs! The KSWs in question were again L55R-bodied KSW6Bs, numbered MW639-60 (RFM 384-405).

The Crosville KSWs wore the green livery, and had standard three-piece destination boxes. However, at an early date, re-paints excluded the upper cream band and, later, reductions were also made to destination displays. The upper-deck seating on the lowbridge KSWs was of the straight-across type in Nos. MW418-27/43-99, but staggered in Nos. MW631-60.

In May 1958, Crosville revised their fleet number prefix system to a more helpful three letter code, not dissimilar to West Yorkshire's or United's, in many cases. Under this scheme, the KSW6Bs became reprefixed DKB (i.e., Double deck, K class, Bristol-engined), while the sole KSW5G became No. DKG428 (note that there was no change to the actual number carried).

Withdrawals of lowbridge KSWs began as early as 1965. Crosville, like United, employed a policy of indiscriminate withdrawals of any examples of a class, irrespective of age, which resulted in the first KSWs going while very many Ks were still actively in service. The KSW5G, No. DKG428, was retired and stored in 1966, but the rest of the highbridge buses lasted until 1968 (except that No. DKB442 went in 1967), by which time all lowbridge KSWs had gone. Ironically, the last Crosville K class buses of all were actually K6Bs!.

*Plate 51:* Crosville's first KSW, No. MW418 (NFM 50), was delivered in mid-1951 and is seen in this picture at Woodside terminus in Birkenhead, on 20th July of that year. The lowbridge KSWs were scattered over virtually the entire Crosville network and, although large numbers were concentrated at Liverpool and the Wirral depots, many examples were to be found far away in North and Mid-Wales. All but one of the lowbridge NFMs were withdrawn at the end of 1965, thereby constituting the first large scale withdrawal of KSWs in the country.

*R. L. Wilson*

Plate 52: Crosville was one of several fleets to take both lowbridge and highbridge KSWs into stock, although they were exceptional in having very many more low-bridge examples than highbridge. The 12in. difference in height between the two variatons is clearly seen in this view of highbridge bus No. MW430 (NFM 62) alongside lowbridge version No. MW418 (NFM 50). The latter had gained the alternative style of radiator filler cap by this time.

*R. F. Mack*

Plate 53: Crosville's highbridge KSWs were allocated primarily for use on the Wirral services, and at Wrexham. One route that was associated with this type for many years was service 1, and No. DKB434 (NFM 66) is shown at Woodside, Birkenhead, after the route had been renumbered C1. The bus illustrates the destination box modifications applied to the type; the majority of KSWs had the 'ultimate' site panelled over, while the rest simply had the glass overpainted. Most buses had a more drastic reduction at the rear, to leave just the route number indicator exposed.

*R. F. Mack*

Plate 54: No fewer than six of the highbridge KSWs, Nos. DKB430/3/4/6/7/9, joined the well-known local fleet of Yates of Runcorn, in 1968. All retained Tilling green livery and their last, No. DKB439, remained in service until November 1973. In this view, the former Nos. DKB434/6 (NFM 66/8) are seen at their depot in June 1969. No. DKB434 clearly shows the bulkhead-mounted Autovac tank, a feature more commonly associated with the K-type. KSs and KSWs were never built with this unit, but Crosville, Bristol and Notts & Derby modified small numbers of their examples in this way.

*Graham Jones*

*Plate 55:* A brand-new KSW6B, No. MW444 (OFM 602) shows the gold fleet number transfers used until fleet number plates were introduced in the mid-1950s. The use of the operator's name in the ultimate destination box was very uncommon in 1952, when No. MW444 was photographed in Chester en route for Llangollen, via Wrexham. Also clearly visible is the recessed quarter panel at lower saloon window level, this being a feature of all KS/KSW buses built prior to the 1954 changes to the rear lights and registration plate.

*R. H. G. Simpson*

*Plate 56:* This view of No. MW478 (OFM 636) again shows a Crosville KSW in original condition, including black lining to the two cream bands. This is something of a contrast to the final appearance of this company's KSWs. Originally, Crosville pre-ferred its intermediate blinds to contain one word, in large letters (as did Wilts & Dorset), rather than the more common three-line display. Many Crosville KSWs were fitted with black steering wheels from new, as can be seen in this view of No. MW478 on a Wirral local service, amid Birkenhead Corporation buses.

*R. F. Mack*

*Plate 57:* Crosville was a pioneer of the practice of omitting the upper cream band on double deckers as they were repainted, KSWs first being treated this way in the mid-1950s. This photograph of No. MW491 (OFM 649) in this condition, shows the bus at the Pier Head in Liverpool, with tram lines and overhead wires still in situ — their last trams ran in 1957. Although the company's KSW fleet totalled more than 100 units, it soon became overshadowed by the vast number of Lodekkas entering service, an early example of which, No. ML670 (RFM 415), one of the 1953 order for 58 LD6Bs, stands beyond the KSW.

*R. F. Mack*

*Plate 58:* In July 1959, Crosville renumbered its routes from a purely numerical sequence to one combining an area prefix letter with numbers. Here, one of the 1953 batch, No. DKB641 (RFM 386), is seen at the Pier Head, Liverpool, in the fairly short-lived period during which the renumbered routes retained intermediate displays — the panelling-down of destination boxes was not far away!

*R. H. G. Simpson*

*Plate 59:* This view, of two of the last KSWs delivered to Crosville, was taken at Rock Ferry Depot in May 1964, and shows the final condition of the company's KSWs. The buses are Nos. DKB657 and DKB659 (RFM 402/4), and the picture shows the bulkhead-mounted fleet number plates, introduced circa 1959/60. Crosville was one of the few firms never to fit flashing trafficators to KSWs and, indeed, many Lodekkas were never afforded what we would nowadays term a necessity. Both KSWs here have been equipped with Autovac tanks.

*Geoff Stainthorpe*

# EASTERN COUNTIES

The predominantly flat terrain of East Anglia had a major effect on the fleet content of Eastern Counties Omnibus Company, principally in that the company could utilise the 5 cylinder Gardner engine widely, although some 6 cylinder Bristol-engined double deckers were obtained for the more hilly regions. Highbridge bodywork was more common than the lowbridge type in this fleet.

The company was a descendant of United Automobile Services Ltd., and the fleet number prefix system was still based on an old United system, in which 'L' was the code letter for Bristols. On the K class buses, a second letter 'K' was carried, with the additional letter 'H' for highbridge examples. There was no duplication of actual numbers.

Against the 1950 order, four Ks and twenty six KSs were built. Nos. LK276-9 (LNG 276-9) were K5Gs with L55R bodies, Nos. LK280-94 (LNG 280-94) were KS5Gs, also with L55R bodywork, while Nos. LK295-300 (LNG 295-300) had 8ft. wide L55R bodies on the same chassis type. Additionally, there were Nos. LKH261-5 (LNG 261-5), which had KS6B chassis and highbridge bodies of 8ft. width.

KSWs appeared in 1951 in the form of Nos. LK301-5 (MAH 301-5), L55R-bodied KSW6Bs — the last lowbridge buses to be delivered, it transpired — and Nos. LKH266-75 (LNG 266-75) and Nos.LKH306-32 (MAH 306-32), all H6OR-bodied KSW5Gs (except for Nos. LKH272-4, which were KSW6Bs). This made an impressive total of forty two machines.

A mere ten highbridge KSW5Gs arrived in 1952, namely Nos. LKH333-42 (NAH 933-42), then in 1953, a final batch of eight similar machines materialised as Nos. LKH166-73 (OVF 166-73), to be followed shortly by the first Lodekkas.

Whereas United Automobile Services converted their KSW5Gs to KSW6Bs, Eastern Counties did exactly the opposite. In 1953, the three highbridge KSW6Bs, Nos. LKH272-4, were re-engined, then between 1955 and 1958 the highbridge 8ft. KS6Bs, Nos. LKH261-5 became KS5Gs. The re-engining of Nos. LK301-5 from 6B to 5G took place between 1955 and 1959, resulting in all KSs and KSWs now being 5LW-powered. The fleet was of standard design and carried red livery (including black lining to the cream bands — a great asset). In 1965, many of the later KSWs received destination box modifications, and combined rear light clusters were fitted to Nos. LK301/5, and to the entire surviving highbridge fleet in 1967.

In January 1968, the company acquired two second-hand KSWs! These were open-top KSW5Gs from the Eastern National fleet (q.v.), and they were placed in service at Felixstowe during that summer. They were numbered LKO238/9 (WNO 481/2, ex-Eastern National Nos. 2385/1). The withdrawal of the lowbridge KSs took place during 1966/7, with the five lowbridge KSWs following in 1968. Whereas the first highbridge KSs were sold during 1968/9, most of the highbridge KSW fleet lasted intact until 1970, but was cleared by 1971. There were, however, two vehicles that went early, for breaking up; No. LKH271 after an accident in 1963, and No. LKH166 with a cracked chassis in 1965. The two open-toppers were withdrawn in 1971, sadly without replacement.

*Plate 60:* Although the double-deck fleet of Eastern Counties was predominantly of highbridge layout, a fleet of lowbridge buses was required at Ipswich area depots, due to insufficient headroom being provided for highbridge buses to enter Ipswich Depot and bus station! No. LK286 (LNG 286), a lowbridge KS5G, was new in October 1950 to Bury St. Edmunds Depot, but was allocated to Ipswich by the time this photograph was taken outside the depot in April 1964.

*Maurice Doggett*

*Plate 61:* The 8ft. wide body on the narrower KS chassis is most apparent in this view. No. LKH265 (LNG 265) was new as a KS6B, with its 'straight' registration plate mounted at the foot of the radiator, as most commonly associated with Western/Southern National. Later, the plate was resited on the cab dash, as shown, and, in 1958, the bus was re-engined with a Gardner 5LW unit. All five buses of this batch spent their entire lives at Norwich and No. LKH265 is seen in Castle Meadow on 14th June 1965. This bus eventually became the last KS to run for Eastern Counties, being withdrawn in March 1970.

*Maurice Doggett*

*Plate 62:* Eastern Counties had the most varied KS fleet of any company, as the only type missing from the four KS variations was the high-bridge 7ft. 6in. bus. The lowbridge 8ft. example illustrated, No. LK296 (LNG 296), was another bus to be allocated to Ipswich for many years and, indeed, doubled up as that depot's driver trainer. When employed on these duties, the vehicle carried a slipboard, which was mounted in the small brackets seen at the top of the radiator. No. LK296 also displays the style of fleetname used until the mid-1950s.

*R. F. Mack*

*Plate 63:* The five lowbridge KSWs, Nos. LK301-5 (MAH 301-5), were originally to be found as far apart as King's Lynn, Cambridge and Bury St. Edmunds, and were not associated with Ipswich, apart from rare loans. No. LK305 was allocated to Bury St. Edmunds for its entire life (apart from one month at Ipswich) and is seen at the bus station in April 1964, displaying the later style of fleetname. Originally Bristol-engined, a Gardner 5LW had been installed in 1957. This bus, jointly with No. LK304, was the last lowbridge double decker to work for Eastern Counties, being withdrawn at the end of September 1968.

*Maurice Doggett*

*Plate 64:* Another KSW6B to be re-equipped with a Gardner 5LW motor was No. LKH274 (LNG 274), which was dealt with as early as 1953. It was one of the first ten highbridge KSWs delivered in 1951, and which continued the LNG registration series of the 1950 order. Norwich depot possessed a large proportion of the highbridge KSWs for use on city services, and No. LKH274 is seen near All Saints Church in June 1969, still retaining the black lining to the cream bands. Around this time, second-hand LS single deckers were being acquired by Eastern Counties from several other former BTC companies, and LS6G XNU 420, seen astern of the KSW, had just arrived from Midland General.

*Graham Jones*

*Plate 65:* Cambridge also possessed several highbridge KSWs for their city services. No. LKH312 (MAH 312) is seen at the railway station in June 1969 and displays a full set of linens, the three-line 'via' display becoming somewhat of a rarity by that date. Indeed, its retention is somewhat surprising, in view of the modifications carried out to some of the class since 1965 *(see Plate 66)*. Eastern Counties was one of the companies that fitted flashing trafficators on the lower cream band of its KSWs, a position more readily associated with Lodekkas.

*Graham Jones*

*Plate 66:* In 1965, many of Eastern Counties' later highbridge KSWs had their front and rear ultimate destination sites panelled over, to conform with the style that had been standard on new stock since as early as 1956. Those so treated were Nos. LKH319/29/31-3/5-42 and LKH166/7/9-72. No. LKH338 (NAH 938), a member of the 1952 order, is seen at Thorpe Station, Norwich, in June 1969.

*Graham Jones*

*Plate 67:* Every single KSW to be built, and all but twelve of the KSs had, of course, visited Lowestoft. However, the Eastern Counties depot in the town never housed more than a handful of these models. No. LKH173 (OVF 173), which was the last KSW to enter service with Eastern Counties (on 1st January 1954), did spend most of the 1960s based there, and the bus is seen in June 1965, on a local service.

*Maurice Doggett*

*Plate 68:* Two open-top KSW5Gs were acquired from Eastern National in 1968, and were numbered LKO238/9 (WNO 481/2). Both worked the coastal service 248 at Felixstowe in the summer of 1968, and No. LKO238 is seen at the top of the steep rise near the Pier, in this picture taken in August of that year. No. LKO239 was placed at Cromer for the 1969 and 1970 summers, while No. LKO238 remained at Felixstowe for 1969, before moving to Great Yarmouth in 1970, to act as relief on normal routes! Sadly, both open-toppers were withdrawn after Derby Day duties in June 1971 (Eastern Counties were not to try open-top operations again until 1978). The bus shown subsequently became well-known as the much-travelled Tricentrol bus *(see Plate 81)*.

*G. R. Mills*

The history of the Eastern National KS and KSW fleet is complex to relate, yet most interesting, as it was greatly affected by the plans of the newly-formed British Transport Commission for the rationalisation of operators' areas. Until these plans were put into effect, the two Essex-based ex-Tilling operators were entirely separate concerns.

Eastern National's double deckers were primarily 5LW-engined lowbridge machines, and orders after 1950 continued this policy. The 1950 order itself called for a mere seven KS5Gs, which were numbered 4111-7 (RPU 521-7). The 1951 order was somewhat larger, calling for 33 KSW5Gs. These became Nos. 4118-20 (SHK 511-3) and Nos. 4136-65 (SHK 518-29, TNO 673-90). Thirty five more KSW5Gs were ordered for 1952, but the area changes took place before delivery was made.

Westcliff-on-Sea Motor Services was a small operator running red buses in Southend and Westcliff, in the Thames estuary holiday area. Again an all-lowbridge fleet, 5LW-engined buses predominated, but there were a few with Bristol engines.

Five KSs were delivered in 1950 — three KS5Gs and two KS6Bs. Westcliff vehicles had no fleet numbers, reference being made by their registrations. These KSs were DJN 554/6-9, the last two being the KS6Bs. The 1951 order consisted of one KSW6B (DJN 560), and six KSW5Gs (EJN 627-32). For 1952, another six KSW5Gs were ordered, and these eventually materialised as FJN 156-61.

However, 1952 was a year of great change. Under BTC direction, Eastern National's geographically separate 'Midland' region, around Luton and Bedford, was transferred lock, stock and barrel to United Counties Omnibus Co. Ltd. This involved the transfer of some 235 vehicles, which included five of the seven KSs, and nine KSWs. The vehicles concerned were Nos. 4111/2/5-8/37/8/42/5/8/9/52/3, which became United Counties vehicles Nos. 825-9 (KSs) and 875-83 (KSWs), with effect from 1st May (q.v.).

Shortly after the loss of the Midland Region, Eastern National gained control of Westcliff-on-Sea and, as an initial move, one of the first KSWs of Eastern National's new order, UEV 830, which was intended to become No. 4175, was diverted to Westcliff, where it entered service in green livery, it is believed, but with Westcliff names and no fleet numbers.

UEV 831-9 became Eastern National Nos. 4176-84, but UEV 840-2, together with UVX 664-6, were further Westcliff buses. Eastern National then took Nos. 4185-95 and 4203 (VNO 855-66), whilst Westcliff received VNO 867/8, just after taking their last two FJNs. Another five buses from this order were delivered directly to United Counties as their Nos. 917-21 (HNV 733-7).

Eastern National's Nos. 4188-90 were interesting, as they had platform doors, and were the only Eastern National KSWs with this feature. Furthermore, they had staggered seating on the upper deck.

Before being taken over, Westcliff ordered six more KSW5Gs, for 1953 but, on building, these were fully integrated with Eastern National's order for eight similar machines, and were identifiable only by the separate sequence of body numbers. When it came to delivery, the totals for the two concerns were reversed, Westcliff receiving eight (WNO 472-9, of which the first four had Eastern National body numbers), and the National six, Nos. 4204-7/15/6

(WNO 482-5/80/1), the last two being from the Westcliff order. All had staggered upper-deck seating, and were the last KSWs for either fleet.

Due to the changes that had overcome the Eastern National fleet, it was decided to undertake a complete fleet numbering on 18th July 1954, now incorporating the Westcliff vehicles. Bristol double deckers were renumbered in a series from 1101, in approximate chassis number order. The KSs and KSWs became Nos. 1343-1430 (88 buses). Of the Eastern National buses, the remaining KSs became Nos. 1348/9, the remaining SHKs became Nos. 1351-60 and TNOs, Nos. 1364-6/9-79, in order. Then Nos. 4176-95 and 4203 were renumbered 1381-5/8-91 (UEV), 1401/3/2/6-14 (VNO). The WNOs, Nos. 4204-7/15/6 became Nos. 1424/5/9/30/27/8 respectively.

Ex-Westcliff KSs took the numbers 1343-7, their KSW6B took 1350, then the EJNs became 1361-3/7/8/80 (a fault of the system showed up here, as No. 1368 and No. 1380 had consecutive chassis numbers!); the FJNs became Nos. 1386/7/92/3, 1404/5. The UEV/UVX/VNO batch became Nos. 1394-1400/15/6, the WNOs becoming 1417/8/21/2/19/20/23/6 respectively. The red Westcliff livery eventually disappeared, and some buses were reallocated in the Eastern National territory.

Ten years after the 1954 numbering, by which time the Eastern National fleet had attained a great degree of standardisation, another fleet renumbering took place, each class having its own series. Under this scheme, the KSs and KSWs took the 2300 series (a unique case of KSs and KSWs being numbered separately from Ks). The renumbering, on 8th August 1964, was straightforward this time, Nos. 1343-1430 becoming 2300-2387.

Eastern National's operational area includes a number of holiday resorts and one of the popular features of major seaside towns, such as Southend and Clacton, is the open-top bus. During the winter of 1965/6, Eastern National decided to replace its fleet of Leylands by rebuilding some KSWs. The last ten KSWs in the fleet list were chosen, namely Nos. 2378-2387. The rebuilding was quite a major operation as, besides losing their roofs, the buses were converted to the highbridge type upper-deck layout (seating 33 passengers; the seats being transferred from the Leylands), and the sunken offside gangway removed. Windshields were placed round the front of the upper deck, and T-type destination boxes were fitted front and rear (except that Nos. 2378/80/2/4/6 had route numbers only, at the rear). Additional external brightwork was applied, and the new open-toppers received a livery of cream, with green relief.

Withdrawals of standard KSs and KSWs commenced at the end of 1967, and progressed until the last lowbridge buses went at the beginning of 1971. The first of the open-toppers to go were Nos. 2381 and 2385, which were sold in January 1968 to Eastern Counties (q.v.). The withdrawal of six more of the batch was, remarkably, to take a further fourteen years to complete, including the notable disposal of No. 2386 to South Wales Transport (see Plates 162 & 163), thereby leaving just Nos. 2383 and 2384 in Eastern National ownership in 1983. By this time, both buses were licensed only as private vehicles, although a welcome event for 1984 was the repainting of both buses into their former cream and green livery, for continued use at rallies and carnivals etc.

*Plate 69:* This red Westcliff-on-Sea KS5G, registered DJN 557, is seen in its original condition, including black-painted radiator grille and wheels. After the absorption of the Westcliff-on-Sea fleet by Eastern National, this bus was numbered 1345, being renumbered 2302 ten years later, in 1964. Several early KSs were fitted with oblong registration plates across the cab dash, as shown here, other examples being found with Eastern Counties, Eastern National and Thames Valley. DJN 557 is seen on a warm summer's day . . . and they don't make baby carriages like that any more!

*D. S. Giles*

*Plate 70:* Green Eastern National KS5G, No. 4115 (RPU 525) saw only eighteen months' service before being transferred, on 1st May 1952, to United Counties, by whom it was numbered 827. The bus worked from Hitchin Depot, in Hertfordshire, and is seen on 5th April 1952, with less than one month's Eastern National service left. No. 4115 displays the large fleet number plates and huge fleetname that were in use up to the first half of the 1950s.

*Alan B. Cross*

*Plate 71:* New to Westcliff-on-Sea, DJN 558 was a KS6B and one of only three Bristol-engined KS/KSW buses to be run by Eastern National. The bus is seen at Southend, in its final Eastern National condition, as No. 2303, and with masked-out 'via' site to the destination box — a feature applied to many of the class from the mid-1960s. This view also illustrates the standard ENOC practice of painting radiator grilles silver and wheels green, rather than the more usual black, together with the third style of fleetname applied to the class, being of the popular underlined pattern, and small enough to fit into one panel. Clearly noticeable is that black lining was still carried on the cream bands.

*T. Smith*

*Plate 72:* Following the take-over by Eastern National, the red Westcliff-on-Sea buses soon acquired silver-painted radiators, although the wheels remained black, as illustrated by EJN 629. This is one of several instances of the use of a three-line 'via' blind, whereas a two-line display, printed in large lettering, was more common to both operators. In 1954, EJN 629 was numbered 1363 in the ENOC series, and was renumbered 2320 ten years later.

*R. F. Mack*

*Plate 73:* Chelmsford's railway station bridge gave just enough room for lowbridge buses to squeeze through, as illustrated by this 1951 KSW5G, SHK 529, displaying its 'middle' fleet number, 1360 (originally No. 4147, finally No. 2317). It is being pursued by another KSW as it works town service 44A. Clearly visible above the fleet number plate is the small, two letter depot code, which was introduced in 1958. The same system was adopted by Bristol Omnibus Company many years later *(see Plate 49)*.

*R. F. Mack*

*Plate 74:* No. 2326 (TNO 680) is seen on test in Colchester, during October 1964, some two months after being renumbered from 1369. The KSWs from this fleet were always very well-kept, and after withdrawal proved extremely popular with independent operators and private owners. No. 2326 was one such bus, finding further use as transport for an East London Scout Group. Perhaps the greatest fame achieved by Eastern National KSWs after sale, went to VNO 857/62/6 and WNO 476, which were painted red, and took a prominent role in Hammer Films' two comedy productions, 'On The Buses' and 'Mutiny On The Buses', in 1971/2.

*G. R. Mills*

*Plate 75:* An example of an ex-Westcliff KSW transferred away from Southend was No. 2362 (FJN 161) which, in this view, shows the bus to be allocated to Kelvedon, a depot acquired with the independent operator Moore Bros., in 1963. The bus is seen in Braintree on 13th September 1970, in company with a similar KSW5G, the former Wilsts & Dorset No. 346 (HMR 415), by then owned by Ford's Coaches of Althorne, on the occasion of a PSV Circle tour, using the HMR-registered bus. The photograph gives a good comparison between the two canopy styles. It also shows that the destination box on No. 2362 has green masking, instead of black.

*G. R. Mills*

*Plate 76:* Still looking new, UVX 666 proudly displays its Westcliff-on-Sea fleetnames, although again it shows the 'silver grille' influence of Eastern National. It is seen here near Southend railway station, with Corporation trolleybus overhead wires still in existence (the system was abandoned in October 1954). The destination blind is somewhat out of date in quoting 'LMS' (the London, Midland & Scottish Railway became the London Midland Region of British Railways on nationalisation in 1948)! The Westcliff-on-Sea routes were soon to be renumbered, following the introduction of the Southend area pooling agreement of 1953.

*R. F. Mack*

*Plate 77:* In the spring of 1953, three KSWs with platform doors, VNO 858-60 (originally numbered 4188-90), entered service from Braintree Depot, on the busy route 322 to London (King's Cross). This route had previously been operated by Hicks Bros., who came under Eastern National control on 1st January 1950, but as the services and licences were not transferred until 1954, the three KSWs originally carried 'On hire to Hicks Bros.' on the front bulkhead. Although fitted with platform doors and heaters, the buses had 5LW Gardner engines, with 4 speed gearboxes and bus seats, an odd choice for such a prestigious London service! No. 1408 (VNO 860), seen at King's Cross, displays the smaller pattern of block fleetname (*see Plates 70 & 71*).

*R. H. G. Simpson*

*Plate 78:* Among Eastern National's ten open-top conversions could be found two distinct variations of detail finish. No. 2379 (WNO 475), shown here, illustrates the type with a curved base line to the upper-deck front windows and 'flared' side screen glazing. The fleetname panel, beneath the downstairs window, does not have a lower strip of brightwork running towards the rear of the bus, either. For the 1966-73 seasons, Clacton regularly saw two or three open-top KSWs allocated for service 112. In this photograph, taken in August 1968, No. 2379 arrives at Jaywick, and shows the single-track route number blind and the green background for the fleetname. Other Clacton open-toppers included Nos. 2381/5 (WNO 482/1), the two buses sold, early in 1968, to Eastern Counties (*see Plate 68*), and these were consequently the only ones never to see service at Southend.

*G. R. Mills*

*Plate 79:* The other variation of the open-top conversion involved squarer upper-deck front windows and a shorter side window. An additional strip of brightwork ran rearwards from the fleetname panel. Also, the polished beading at upper-deck floor level dropped distinctly between the front of the bus and bulkhead level, as seen on No. 2382 (WNO 483). The principal stage on which Eastern National's open-toppers performed was at Southend, where, in addition to route 67, they could also be found on Southend Corporation's service 68. The hiring of these buses to the Corporation became a regular feature and, indeed, during a couple of seasons, the KSWs only saw Corporation service, due to severe Eastern National staff shortages, No. 2382 was photographed on the Corporation service in June 1969, having just passed beneath Southend's famous pier. There was a requirement for all open-toppers to stop before going below the pier, and for the conductor to check all passengers were seated before proceeding, due to the restricted headroom.

*Graham Jones*

*Plate 80:* By 1974, the operational fleet of open-top KSWs was down to just four buses, namely Nos. 2379/82-4 (WNO 475/83/79/80). However, in that year, their cream and Tilling green livery was superseded by NBC white, with leaf green relief, which now included the waistband. The former fleetname panel and the lower strip of brightwork were removed, to enable standard NBC pattern fleetnames and logos to be applied. The rear route indicators were also removed. All four buses were kept in immaculate condition for service 67 at Southend or, occasionally, service 112 at Clacton, and in 1977, No. 2382 was further 'customised' by enthusiastic ENOC staff, as can be seen, and the bus became very well-known at rallies. Sadly, this bus was completely destroyed by fire at Prittlewell Works in August 1981. In happier days, No. 2382 is seen here at Southend Pier on 16th August 1978.

*Allan Macfarlane*

*Plate 81:* As recorded, WNO 481/2 had only a short life as open-toppers with Eastern National and a not very much longer life with Eastern Counties (*see Plate 68*). However, they were quickly purchased by independent operators. By far the most widely-travelled of the pair proved to be WNO 481, which passed to Hall of Hounslow. It was then used as an accommodation bus for Paul McCartney's 'Wings' pop group to tour Scandinavia, during 1972, with most of its seats removed. Subsequently, the bus came under Tricentrol control, and was painted in a mustard and white livery, all seats having been re-upholstered and restored. The bus has been a familiar entry at bus rallies ever since, and has even ventured abroad again, in 1980, to attend the Tulip Bus Rally in Holland. In this picture, WNO 481 looks at home on an English 'prom', not at Clacton, but at Brighton, in April 1974.

*Allan Macfarlane*

*Plate 82:* When Eastern National was faced with a surplus of open-toppers, it found these vehicles made ideal tree-loppers . . . not surprisingly. The first treated, No. 2387, enjoyed only two years of open-top passenger service before becoming tree-lopper No. 0485 (WNO 485), in 1968. Again its life in this form was to be relatively short, as the bus was replaced early in 1973 by sister machine No. 2378, which was renumbered 0474 (WNO 474), and this bus is seen in February of that year, at Colchester. It makes an interesting comparison with Bristol Omnibus Company's No. W120, seen in *Plate 33*. No. 0474 was sold in 1976.

*G. R. Mills*

# HANTS & DORSET

The KSWs of Hants & Dorset always had an individual appearance; this was due to the buses having visors over their windscreens and registration plates at the foot of the radiator.

Seventeen KSs (six of which were 8ft. wide) and 52 KSWs were delivered to Hants & Dorset in three batches. The 1950 order was unusual in that examples of the K-type appeared in the same batch as the KSs and KSWs (eleven vehicles, Nos. 1257-67, KEL 700-10, lowbridge K6Bs). The KSs commenced with Nos. 1268-78 (KEL 711-21), also with L55R bodies changing to 8ft. wide KSs for Nos. 1279-84 (KEL 722-7) and finally to KSWs for the remaining three members of the batch, Nos. 1285-87 (KEL 728-30). All were AVW-powered. The 1951 order materialised as Nos. 1288-98 (KRU 954-64), L55R-bodied KSW6Bs, and H6OR-bodied KSW6Bs Nos. 1299-1321 (KRU 965-87). The latter were interesting, as only nineteen highbridge buses had appeared in the fleet beforehand, delivered between 1929 and 1948! For 1952, highbridge KSWs were again specified: Nos. 1322/3 (LRU 51/2) were KSW6Bs, but the rest of the batch were KSW6Gs, these being Nos. 1324-36 (LRU 53-65). For 1953, and subsequent years, Hants & Dorset chose to buy the Lodekka.

However, mention must be made of a batch of pre-war K5Gs that Hants & Dorset had rebodied by ECW in 1954. The bodies were 8ft. wide highbridge 60 seaters and, except for being slightly shorter in the bonnet and platform sections, were to the KSW design. The buses concerned were Nos. 1013 (BTR 303), 1024/30/1/3 (JT 9352/8/9/61), 1034/5/51

(ERU 262/586/602) and 1083/6 (FLJ 535/8), and of these Nos. 1013/34/5/51/83/6 were convertible to open-top, an unusual feature in 1954, and were painted cream. No. 1086 lost its detachable roof under a low bridge in 1960, by which time all were painted in standard bus livery, although No. 1086 reverted to cream in 1962. The batch was withdrawn by 1964, No. 1086 passing to Southern Vectis (q.v.).

Hants & Dorset buses carried the green livery, although the upper cream band on the double deckers was eliminated from the early 1960s. A few of the final KSW repaints also received green instead of black wings.

In 1971, two years after the merger of the management of Wilts & Dorset with that of Hants & Dorset, the company introduced parallel fleet numbering schemes for the two fleets. Hants & Dorset's remaining KSs and KSWs were numbered up to 1399, thus KSs Nos. 1270/2/4-6/8-83 were allocated the numbers 1338-48, lowbridge KSWs Nos. 1286-98 became 1349-61, and highbridge KSWs Nos. 1299-1336 became 1362-99. However, some vehicles, notably the lowbridge examples, were withdrawn before receiving their new numbers.

Withdrawals in general started as late as 1970, and it was not until late 1974 that the type finally departed from public service with Hants & Dorset, by which time some of these vehicles could lay claim to several entries in the KS/KSW record book.

*Plate 83:* As was the case in many fleets, Hants & Dorset's 1950 order included KSs and the company's first KSWs. The difference in width, and in dash styling, is clearly visible in this view of KS6B No. 1271 (KEL 714), standing back from 'big sister' KSW6B No. 1286 (KEL 729), at Southampton Depot, on 5th April 1969. Southampton always had a good cross-section of the lowbridge buses, but was not without the highbridge variety. Both these buses show modifications made since 1962, in that the upper cream band has been eliminated, and the ultimate destination site has been overpainted — a less expensive, if less tidy method of achieving the same results as Crosville, Eastern Counties, etc. *(see Plates 59 & 66).*

*Graham Jones*

*Plate 84:* The eleven Hants & Dorset 7ft. 6in. KS6Bs were a familiar sight in the company's eastern area, for their entire lives — indeed, only Nos. 1268 and 1270 were ever found at the western end of the operator's territory, and even then, only for a short spell at the end of their lives. No. 1272 (KEL 715), seen at Gosport amid Gosport & Fareham Traction buses, was new to Fareham Depot, and stayed there until its last year of service. The batch had the longest life of any company's KSs (No. 1272 itself managed just short of 21 years) and indeed, Hants & Dorset's KSs were the last in passenger service anywhere.

*R. H. G. Simpson*

*Plate 85:* Hants & Dorset's 1950 order was fairly uncommon, by materialising in four variations of length and width! The batch consisted of examples of K, KS, 8ft. KS and KSW buses, all with L55R bodywork. This comparison view of KS6B No. 1277 (KEL 720), standing alongside K6B No. 1257 (KEL 700), illustrates that the differences between the two models were not so pronounced at the back as at the front, particularly in lowbridge form. The enlarged platform window and revised destination boxes, introduced with the KS/KSW class, are the prime differences. The extra strip of beading on the lower rear panels was a Hants & Dorset feature. The fleet number-plates are colour-coded to denote the allocation: No. 1277 has yellow figures and edging to a black plate, for Woolston Depot, while the reversed colours on No. 1257 indicates that Southampton is its base. The photograph was taken at Woolston, in August 1968.

*Graham Jones*

*Plate 86:* The only Hants & Dorset KSW to become a fully-fledged driver trainer was No. 1285 (KEL 728), their first KSW model, which was converted in January 1970. The modifications included the cutting away of most of the offside front bulkhead, the removal of the upper-deck seats, the installation of weights to simulate passenger loads, and the fitment of platform doors. No emergency door was required, as the bus was not licensed for public use. It retained Tilling green livery and its original fleet number, until being renumbered 9099, in an ancilliary vehicle series, in the 1971 scheme. It was photographed at Bournemouth, its home base, in June 1972 and remained in use until August 1975. It will be noted that the quarter panel at lower-deck window level has been glazed — only Hants & Dorset and Bristol bothered to glaze this panel on the 1950/1 order buses (see Plate 19).

*P. J. Relf*

*Plate 87:* Although most Hants & Dorset K class buses had their registration plates transferred to the foot of the radiator, the six 8ft. KSs, Nos. 1279-84, were actually delivered in that condition, as were, of course, examples for other fleets (*see Plates 147 & 192 for example*). No. 1282 (KEL 725) spent its entire life at Southampton and was photographed leaving the bus station, during April 1969, on a route that ran entirely within the Southampton city boundary, yet was not the responsibility of Southampton Corporation Transport.

*Graham Jones*

*Plate 88:* This KSW doesn't really look like a Hants & Dorset bus! Photographed on 16th October 1951, when little over one month old, No. 1294 (KRU 960) has yet to receive a visor above the windscreen, or to have the registration plate replaced by one on the radiator. It is shown at the old Bournemouth bus station and, although several of the lowbridge buses were new to Bournemouth and Poole depots, all had gone to Southampton and Fareham by 1952, not to return to the western area until the 1960s. The fleet number plates, introduced in 1950, were originally black, with polished figures and edges, as seen here. The colour coding (*see Plate 85*) was not introduced until 1956.

*P. J. Relf*

*Plate 89:* Following the 1971 fleet numbering scheme, few lowbridge buses remained in service to carry their new numbers. One that survived was KRU 964, the last lowbridge bus to arrive with Hants & Dorset. It was renumbered from 1298 to 1361, but was withdrawn in 1972. However, in May 1973, it was reinstated, as one of three KSWs (each different in specification!) to be placed at Winchester, in the wake of Hants & Dorset's take-over of the independent 'King Alfred' fleet of R. Chisnell & Sons. The other two KSWs were No. 1384 (KRU 987), a highbridge KSW6B (seen to the rear of No. 1361), and Wilts & Dorset No. 371 (HMW 448), a red, lowbridge KSW5G. The buses were employed on former 'King Alfred' town services, as shown by No. 1361, seen at the Broadway, on route 15. The date is 20th June, and when No. 1361 was withdrawn at the end of October 1973, it had become the last green lowbridge KSW, and the last lowbridge KSW6B, to run in public service within the NBC. The surviving lowbridge buses were Wilts & Dorset KSW5Gs, themselves owned by Hants & Dorset.

*Graham Jones*

*Plate 90:* Hants & Dorset's highbridge KSWs were particularly associated with the Bournemouth and Poole area. They were the mainstay of the very intensive group of services operated between the two towns, right through to the late 1960s. No. 1312 (KRU 978) is seen in mid-1950s condition (still with a dash-mounted registration plate) passing through Bournemouth Square. Its fleet number colour indicates that it is one of many of the batch to work from Parkstone Depot. After the operational closure of this depot in 1958, Poole housed virtually all from Nos. 1299-1321.

*R. H. G. Simpson*

*Plate 91:* In what many will remember as typical 1960s condition is No. 1299 (KRU 965), which makes an interesting comparison with No. 1312 in the previous plate. The distinctive gold 'H' transfer, denoting highbridge vehicles, remained with these buses throughout their lives and it can clearly be seen beneath the front fleet number. No. 1299 received a repaint late in life, as illustrated by this July 1969 view at Bournemouth bus station. An FS6B Lodekka, No. 1492 (4692 RU) is seen behind, working another of the routes to Poole. Sadly, this famous bus station has now finally been demolished, in the aftermath of the disastrous fire of 1976.

*Graham Jones*

*Plate 92:* A classic portrait of a Hants & Dorset KSW! The highbridge KSW6Gs of this fleet were more commonly found at the eastern area depots. Both Winchester and Southampton had examples allocated, and they were regularly used on the busy route 47, which linked the two towns. It was one of few routes in the area that did not incur low bridges. No. 1330 (LRU 59) arrives at Southampton on 16th May 1959. Note that Hants & Dorset, like Westcliff-on-Sea and Eastern National, preferred a two-line intermediate blind.

*G. Mead*

*Plate 93:* A handful of highbridge KSWs survived long enough with Hants & Dorset to receive green painted wings and NBC style fleet-names (in cream lettering), as illustrated by No. 1394 (LRU 60 and formerly No. 1331), at Fareham bus station in May 1973. LRU 60 and LRU 61 both spent their entire lives at Fareham Depot, totalling 21 and 22 years respectively! With the notable exception of several KSW6Gs remaining with Bristol Omnibus Company, LRU 61, at the time of its withdrawal, in November 1974, was the last closed-top KSW in service with an NBC fleet.

*Allan Macfarlane*

*Plate 94:* Three of Hants & Dorset's buses became the last KSW6Bs in NBC service. All were withdrawn in February 1974, and included No. 1375 (KRU 978 — *see Plate 90*), which is shown at Poole bus station in March 1973. This picture again shows the extra strip of beading on the lower rear panel — an aid to accident damage replacement. It also shows the fleet number transfers and self-adhesive coloured stickers used for depot codes, both introduced at the 1971 fleet numbering.

*Allan Macfarlane*

*Plate 95:* Of the ten pre-war K5Gs which Hants & Dorset had fitted with new KSW-pattern bodies in 1954, the most interesting life was afforded to No. 1086 (FLJ 538). It was one of six whose new bodies were convertible to open-top, and which were painted all cream, apart from green wings, wheels and radiator grille. It is pictured at Fareham, in winter guise. The six only ran in open-top form in the summers of 1954-1958, after which they were repainted in standard green bus livery. In 1960, this vehicle sustained major roof damage under Fareham's dreaded railway arch, and subsequently ran as a permanent open-topper at Poole, in 1961, retaining the green livery, one of only two green examples to see open-top work (*see Plate 96*). In 1962, however, cream livery was restored to this bus alone, and it was reallocated to the Southampton Docks tour. Withdrawal of the ten 1954 rebodied versions commenced as early as 1962, and was completed with the departure of No. 1086, after the 1964 season. Happily, No. 1086 was to enjoy ten more summers, in the ownership of Southern Vectis (*see Plate 114*).

*R. F. Mack*

*Plate 96:* The oldest of the ten pre-war K5Gs to receive new KSW style bodies in 1954 was a 1938 bus, No. 1013 (BTR 303) which was registered in Southampton in the days that Hants & Dorset obtained marks from three authorities, Bournemouth and Dorset being the others. In its cream-liveried seasons, No. 1013 shared, with No. 1086, the Gosport, Lee-on-Solent and Hill Head service 72, the other four running from Poole, to Sandbanks (32) or Rockley Sands (33A). No. 1013, in this view represents the buses after they received green livery during 1958/9, but its convertible nature is still detectable by the lifting lugs on the side of the roof, and by the shallower upper-deck windows. This bus was used in green open-top form for a Southampton Docks tour from 1961, until the tour was left in the hands of No. 1086. The bus shown was sold in 1963; its chassis had seen 25 years service, but this body was only nine years old. Brighton, Hove & District and York-West Yorkshire had similar style highbridge bodies placed on elderly K-type chassis (*see Plates 12, 13, 175 & 176*), but only Hants & Dorset's were 8ft. wide.

*R. F. Mack*

# LINCOLNSHIRE

Operating in one of the flattest counties in Britain, Lincolnshire Road Car Company served relatively sparsely-populated countryside. Despite this, the company once came under BET administration, but was passed to the Tilling group in 1942. The BET influence was slow to pass (some post-war Ks and Ls had BET-style destination boxes), but with the coming of the KSs and KSWs, the transformation to Tilling could be said to be complete. Lincolnshire was not greatly troubled by low bridges, so an all-highbridge fleet of Bristol double deckers was operated.

The company owned a total of only ten KS and KSW buses. The first arrivals, in 1950, were three KS6Bs with H6OR bodies, Nos. 776-8 (GFW 277-9). No buses were ordered for 1951, but in 1952 Lincolnshire took five KSWs. These, numbered 969-73 (JBE 868-72), had Gardner 6LW engines and platform doors. (Incidentally, the fleet numbering scheme was common to double deckers, saloons and coaches, and on reaching No. 799, it skipped to 951). In 1953, two more KSW6Gs with H6ORD bodies arrived; Nos. 989/90 (KBE 180/1), but after this the company specified the Lodekka. The KSs and KSWs had standard three-piece destination boxes, wore Tilling green livery including black lining-out, and always presented a smart appearance. In 1953, Lincolnshire renumbered its fleet, each class of Bristol having its own block of 100. The K class was numbered into the 2100s, thus KS6Bs Nos. 776-8 became Nos. 2129-31, KSW6Gs Nos. 969-73/89/90 becoming Nos. 2137-43.

Withdrawal of the KSs took place in 1965, and in 1966 all seven KSWs were withdrawn, after a rather short life, by many standards.

*Plate 97:* In addition to the twenty nine examples with Bristol Tramways, the only other green-liveried 7ft. 6in. wide highbridge KSs were three buses with Lincolnshire — GFW 277-9. They were originally numbered 776-8, but became Nos. 2129-31 in 1953. For many years, they were based at Boston and Holbeach depots and regularly appeared on route 65, crossing the girder-section Sutton Bridge and on to reach Eastern Counties' territory at King's Lynn. No. 2131 is seen at the Library terminus at King's Lynn in this February 1962 view.

*Geoff Stainthorpe*

*Plate 98:* Highbridge KSWs with platform doors were only to be found in three fleets and, again, apart from Bristol's, the only green examples were with Lincolnshire! Although constituting only a very small section of the double-deck fleet, KSWs were familiar buses at both Grantham and Newark depots. No. 2138 (JBE 869) is pictured at Grantham bus station, awaiting service between the two towns. Fleet number plates have yet to be fitted.

*R. H. G. Simpson*

*Plate 99:* When Lincolnshire dispensed with 'via' points on destination blinds, a very neat scaled-down version of their fleetname was inserted on to the linens, instead of the less attractive masking or panelling. Lincolnshire's buses had a reputation for their well-kept condition, and an immaculate No. 2140 (JBE 871) is seen at Grantham bus station on 20th July 1963.

*G. R. Mills*

*Plate 100:* Whilst the 1952 KSW order had four speed gearboxes, the two 1953 buses were equipped with five speed boxes. Like their Crosville counterparts, Lincolnshire's KSWs were never fitted with flashing trafficators. No. 2143 (KBE 181) is pictured leaving Grantham bus station. This bus was withdrawn after exactly thirteen years of service, a short life for such a fine machine, and by September 1966, Lincolnshire had become the first former BTC fleet to withdraw its entire K family vehicles

*R. F. Mack*

# NOTTS & DERBY
## TRACTION CO

The Nottinghamshire & Derbyshire Traction Company will be well remembered for running inter-urban trolleybus services between Nottingham and Ripley, a distance of some sixteen miles. The company had begun by operating trams before World War I, and when feeder bus services were started in 1920, the title Midland General was brought into use for the motor vehicles. The two companies, together with the neighbouring Mansfield District Traction Company, became owned by the Midland Counties Electricity Supply Company and, in 1948, when all electricity companies underwent nationalisation, the Midland General group passed into state ownership. The new British Electricity Authority handed over these bus operators to the British Transport Commission.

It was to be a few years before standard BTC Bristol/ECW buses appeared with the Midland General group, and the first instance was as a result of Notts & Derby's decision to abandon its famous trolleybus system. As replacements for half the trolleybus fleet, fifteen KSW6Gs with H60R bodies were delivered in 1953. Starting a new numbering series for Notts & Derby buses, the KSWs became Nos. 300-14 (SRB 528-42). All fifteen had consecutive chassis numbers (98.014-28) — just one of the unusual aspects of this fleet. It was, however, the livery and fittings which made these KSWs exceptional, for they carried the superb blue and cream colours which Midland General and Notts & Derby succeeded in retaining, despite BTC control.

Midland General's 'independent' policy also dictated the unusual pattern of destination boxes and seats. Although carrying three-piece screens (front and rear), the aperture dimensions varied from the standard Tilling pattern. The route number box was equipped with a single track blind. The seats were non-standard, in having a curved top and, in the lower saloon, they were upholstered in MGOC blue moquette, while those in the upper saloon were covered in blue leather, to enable easy cleaning. Indeed, a notice on the platform requested miners in overalls to use only the upper saloon. The main interior colour scheme was, of course, blue, but red was carried on the window pillars, etc. The buses were equipped with Clayton heaters, with the lower-deck outlet in the form of trunking on the front bulkhead. They also, of course, had open platforms.

The Midland General Group took no more KSWs into stock, as they standardised thereafter on Lodekkas (which were similarly equipped and painted). However, mention should be made that in 1955, a batch of six Midland General wartime Guy Arab IIs, Nos. 102-7 (JNU 680-5), and one of Notts & Derby's ex-Mansfield District 1948 AEC Regent IIIs, No. 316 (JVO 942), were rebodied by ECW. These new H32/26R bodies were very much of KS pattern, but were of five-bay construction.

The KSWs had an uncomplicated life with Notts & Derby, the only major event being a renumbering. In January 1968, to make way for new vehicles, the KSWs were renumbered 400-14. However, by the following January, the whole fleet had been withdrawn.

*Plate 101:* This view of Notts & Derby No. 300 (SRB 528), by Eastern Coach Works, clearly shows the application of the blue and cream livery. Notts & Derby's KSWs were alone in being built without the beading to contain an upper cream band, although it was never utilised by Brighton, Hove & District and Cheltenham District. The blue wheels are clearly discernible in this view, as are the curved tops to the seats and the distinctive destination layout.

*Courtesy ECW*

*Plate 102:* The fifteen Notts & Derby KSWs operated from two garages; the former trolleybus depot at Langley Mill and from Midland General's Ilkeston Depot. No. 309 (SRB 537) is pictured at Ilkeston on 1st July 1967, and its immaculate condition belies its fourteen years of age.

*G. R. Mills*

*Plate 103:* Route A2 was one of the former trolleybus routes, although the termini had been changed slightly by the time that No. 313 (SRB 541) was seen heading through a damp and deserted Ilkeston in May 1965. Most of these buses were withdrawn in the summer of 1968 (vehicles now numbered 400-11), whilst Nos. 412-4 hung on until January 1969.

*C. W. Routh*

*Plate 104:* Regrettably, the first twelve KSWs, withdrawn by Notts & Derby, all went straight for breaking, but Nos. 312-4 were to see further service elsewhere. By far the longest-lived example, and one of few KSWs to see service in Scotland, was No. 314 (SRB 542), which was sold to the well known AA Motor Services in Ayrshire, in February 1969. The bus is shown at Dodds' depot at Troon, in August 1973, and the low-mounted Autovac tank can be seen under the nearside sidelight (*see Plate 54*). This bus was withdrawn by Dodds in 1976 and was subsequently acquired for preservation.

*C. W. Routh*

# ROTHERHAM

In the days before the Tilling group and its manufacturers, Bristol and Eastern Coach Works, were nationalised, Bristol, in particular, enjoyed the custom of a number of municipal and company operators outside the Tilling group. One of the most consistent of the municipal customers was Rotherham Corporation, from industrial South Yorkshire, some distance from any Tilling operator. By the time of the 1947 nationalisation, Rotherham Corporation had placed sufficient orders with Bristol Tramways for new chassis, to ensure supply for a few years. The last batch of twelve double deckers was not commenced until after the K-type had been superseded by the KS. Consequently, these twelve had KS6B chassis, and Rotherham Corporation had the distinction of being the only non-BTC operator to take delivery of KSs. Furthermore, as the bodywork was built at the East Lancs factory at Bridlington, East Yorkshire (formerly the Yorkshire Equipment Company) they were also the only KSs to have bodywork other than by ECW.

Fleet numbers of these unique East Lancs-bodied KS6Bs were 100-111 (FET 800-811), and the chassis were built to the 80th and 82nd sanctions. Rotherham Corporation did not take advantage of the extra length to increase the seating capacity, and the bodies were to a spacious H30/26R layout. They were of five bay construction, which was surprising in view of East Lancs' standardisation on four bay layout since the war, as exemplified by Rotherham's K6Bs. They were painted in the Corporation's attractive livery of blue and buff.

The KSs had a good length of service, as withdrawals did not commence until 1967, and the last examples were not taken out of service until 1969. No. 105 subsequently became a trainer.

*Plate 105:* Rotherham Corporation's dozen KS6Bs joined a fleet of sixteen K6Bs (Nos. 169-178 and 197-202) and several L6Bs that were then in the process of being rebodied as double deckers! All had bodywork by East Lancashire Coach Builders, that on the KSs being built at Bridlington, in East Yorkshire (the chassis, of course, travelled to Bridlington from Brislington!). The busy route 77 was jointly operated by the neighbouring Rotherham, Sheffield and Doncaster Corporations, and the KSs were familiar performers on the service. In this view, No. 106 (FET 806) is seen in Doncaster, on a short working, in August 1961.

*M. Fowler*

*Plate 106:* The livery of Rotherham Corporation's buses was slightly modified later, by the omission of the buff band beneath the upper-deck windows, although, as can be seen, beading had not been carried in this position previously. No. 110 (FET 810) also displays an unusual feature for a Bristol double decker; a sliding cab door.

*R. H. G. Simpson*

# SOUTHERN VECTIS

The Isle of Wight, situated off the south coast of England, is a popular holiday venue, and is blessed with pleasant scenery and fine sandy beaches. The Island is very much geared to tourism, and nowhere is this better illustrated than by the fact that the Island's only major bus operator, Southern Vectis, uses a greatly increased number of buses in summer than it does in winter, to cope with the crowds.

In view of the loadings that the buses were sometimes subjected to, and also the hilly terrain of the Island, it is rather surprising that Southern Vectis standardised on the five cylinder Gardner engine in their K class buses. Twenty eight KS/KSW type buses were operated, and all were lowbridge models with open platforms. They carried the green livery, and had standard destination boxes.

The 1950 order called for five double deckers, but delivery was made up of two chassis types, Ks and KSs. Nos. 738/9 (GDL 711/2) were K5Gs, while Nos. 740-2 (GDL 713-5) were KS5Gs, all with L55R bodies. Southern Vectis had a preference for 7ft. 6in. wide double deckers because of the Island's narrow roads and, therefore, for the 1951 delivery, the company specifically called for more KS5Gs. In so doing, they became one of only two operators to take KSs against the 1951 order, the other being York-West Yorkshire (q.v.). The Vectis buses were Nos. 749-58 (HDL 263-72) — the intervening fleet numbers, for the record, were applied to some second-hand Leyland TD1s — which gave them a total of thirteen KSs.

The first KSWs arrived in 1952, the order for ten becoming Nos. 759-68 (JDL 33-42), L55R-bodied KSW5Gs. Nos. 765-8, incidentally, were fitted with full length luggage racks to the nearside of the lower saloon, 'balancing' the sunken offside gangway. These Southern Vectis buses were the only KSWs known to have this feature, other than Bristol Tramways' ten lowbridge KSWs of similar vintage and the Thames Valley coach examples.

For 1953, five more KSW5Gs were ordered, together with five LD6G Lodekkas. The KSWs were numbered 769-73 (JDL 719-23), and again had the lower saloon luggage racks. These buses also had staggered upper-deck seating, and Nos. 771-3 are on record as having the seats set at an angle.

For subsequent deliveries, Southern Vectis specified the Lodekka and, due to rail closures on the Island, and the need to provide replacement services, they soon built up a sizeable fleet of LDs.

In 1961/2, all the KSWs were fitted with under-seat heaters, although the KSs were not so fitted. The heaters were for the benefit of winter passengers, but for the benefit of summer travellers, Southern Vectis operated some open-top double deckers on coastal routes. Of specific interest to this story was one acquired second-hand in 1964, as it had KSW-style body on a 1940 K5G chassis. Numbered 908, it was FLJ 538, one of the Hants & Dorset examples (No.1086), bearing a 1954 PO6OR8 body. It carried a livery of cream with green wings, and looked exceptionally smart. It ran on the Isle of Wight until 1974.

Due to the drop in traffic in winter months, a large number of buses was delicensed. These were generally the older units of the fleet, so that by the early 1960s, the first KSs and KSWs spent the winter in store, and by the 1965/6 winter, no KSs or KSWs were in service at all during these months.

Withdrawal of the KSs commenced in 1967, the last one going in 1969. The first KSWs also went in 1969. At the time of the famous Isle of Wight Pop Festival in August 1970, just two KSWs were left, but due to the vast crowds that needed to be transported, every available bus was pressed into service. Consequently, four other KSWs were reinstated to help, all six (Nos. 767-9/71-3) being placed on major trunk routes (some of which hadn't seen KSWs for some years), thus releasing FLFs for 'festival' duties. The six KSWs were finally withdrawn at the end of the 1970 season.

*Plate 107:* The earlier style of 'yellow' Southern Vectis fleetname shows up well in this view of KS5G No. 756 (HDL 270). Apart from the main depot at Newport, KSs and KSWs were also based at Shanklin and Ryde, thereby ensuring the model's operation on all Island double-deck routes. No. 756 was a regular bus at Ryde for many years, and is seen working a town service. These ten KSs, which entered service in 1952 (the HDLs), were built with the lower-deck nearside quarter-panel glazed — this can clearly be seen through the lower saloon in this photograph.

*R. H. G. Simpson*

*Plate 108:* Southern Vectis was one of the fleets who displayed the operator's name in the 'via' box, after intermediate blinds were discontinued in 1962, although the style was not as neat as that used by Lincolnshire (*see Plate 99*). No. 741 (GDL 714), one of three KSs to enter service in the summer of 1951, displays this style of blind when seen at Newport bus station on a hot summer's day in August 1964. In the background can be seen the only LS bus delivered to Southern Vectis (JDL 43).

*P. J. Relf*

*Plate 109:* The last lowbridge KSs to be built for any fleet were the HDL buses for Vectis, the last of which entered service in the spring of 1952 (the York-West Yorkshire highbridge buses entered traffic early in 1952, and the only subsequent KSs were the 1957 buses for Brighton, Hove & District). The narrower version was specifically requested, due to the width of many of the Island's roads — indeed, even today, some main roads would be considered unsuitable for VR and Olympian double deckers elsewhere, but on the Island, these vehicles are called upon to work over virtually every route. No. 750 (HDL 264) is pictured working on one of the longest routes, service 12 from Sandown, which ran the breadth of the Island, from east to west.

*R. F. Mack*

*Plate 110:* Route 42, on the western side of the Island, was worked in summer by the open-topper based at Freshwater Depot. During inclement weather, however, a KSW was often substituted. On 8th August 1968, No. 761 (JDL 35) crosses the narrow Yarmouth Harbour bridge, leaving the town and the Lymington Ferry behind. Gold fleet number transfers and depot codes were introduced in 1968, the white dot on No. 761 denoting a Newport allocation, from which Freshwater vehicles were supplied. Ryde was represented by a red dot and Shanklin by a blue dot.

*Graham Jones*

*Plate 111:* The upper-deck passengers on KSW5G No. 766 (JDL 40) show just how restricted their vision could be, due to the low height of the roof line. As with Brighton, Hove & District, fog/spot lamps were not fitted to the KS/KSW fleet, although this was rather surprising due to the rural nature of the Island's routes, and the incidence of sea fog enshrouding the Island. No. 766 is seen leaving Shanklin, with vintage cars in evidence.

*R. H. G. Simpson*

*Plate 112:* No. 771 (JDL 721) displays the very clear fleetname style applied between 1957 and 1962 . . . subsequently, thinner lettering was used, in a duller gold. The company's last five KSWs, the JDL 700s, had staggered seating on the upper deck, and this feature can just be seen in this view taken of No. 771 at Sandown, in May 1959.

*G. Mead*

*Plate 113:* These two KSWs enjoyed a considerable period of use after sale by Vectis in 1970. The well-known independent, Morris of Swansea, painted the vehicles in their distinctive livery of two shades of blue, and cream, and employed them on contract work until 1976. Even then the two were not immediately separated, as they were promptly snapped up by Omnibus Promotions and painted in the London Transport red livery, before export.

*Graham Jones Collection*

*Plate 114:* From this angle looking very much like an open-topped 8ft. KS, No. 908 (FLJ 538) was a pre-war K5G, with a 1954 KSW-pattern convertible open-top body. It was acquired from its original operator, Hants & Dorset, in 1964 (*see Plate 95*). For most of its ten years with Southern Vectis, No. 908 was the open-topper associated with Freshwater Depot and route 42 to Alum Bay (*see Plate 110*). In its last but one season, however, the bus is seen, in July 1973, at Lake, near Sandown, on the more arduous eastern coastal open-top route. Service 47 included a severely graded climb over St. Boniface Down, before descending into Ventnor. The destination linens on Southern Vectis' open-toppers were red.

*P. J. Relf*

# THAMES VALLEY

The KS/KSW fleet of the Thames Valley Traction Co. Ltd. is noteworthy for three reasons; firstly, it contained examples with coach seats; secondly, the company continued to take lowbridge KSWs in preference to Lodekkas as late as 1955; and thirdly, some KSWs were acquired second-hand in the late 1960s. In other respects, however, the fleet was fairly standardised, all examples being AVW-engined, and all buses having open platforms. As delivered, it totalled 15 KSs (all 7ft. 6in.) and 76 KSWs, making it the third largest fleet overall (following Bristol and Crosville).

Delivery commenced in 1950 with L55R-bodied KS6Bs Nos. 586-94 (FMO 968-76). Following these came Nos. 595-600 (FMO 977-82), further KS6Bs, but with bodies fitted with 53 coach seats and enclosed rear platforms, the only KSs with this latter feature, and ordered specially for the London services. The last vehicles to this order, Nos. 601-3 (FMO 983-5) were KSW6Bs with L55R bodies, which were part of the pre-production batch of 25 KSW chassis.

The 1951 order called for seventeen KSW6Bs, which became Nos. 634-50 (GJB 272-88). Of these, Nos. 637-9 were again CL27/26RD coaches.

The 1952 order was solely of KSW6B/L55R specification (Nos. 651-70: HBL 53-72), as was that of 1953; Nos. 694-705 (HMO 840-51). Although the Lodekka was now available, Thames Valley not only ordered none for 1953, but continued to order lowbridge KSWs alone from 1954 (United Counties also took lowbridge KSWs in 1954). This new and, ironically, largest order became Nos. 726-749 (JRX 801-824). Nos. 738-43 were again coaches, while Nos. 744-9, entering service in

1955, became the last lowbridge KSWs to enter service anywhere.

As built, all vehicles had standard triple destination boxes at the front, but most had 'T' boxes at the rear, and carried the red livery with two cream bands. However, as early as 1957, repaints omitted the upper cream band,. Buses numbered 694-705, 725-37 and 744-9 had staggered upper-deck seating.

During 1966, Thames Valley stepped up their famous policy of buying suitable second-hand buses and, although these were usually Lodekkas, initially from United Welsh, the two United Welsh lowbridge KSW6Gs, Nos. 1242/3 (JCY 989/90) were also acquired. Before entering service with Thames Valley, they were converted to KSW6B, numbered 672/3 (numbers vacated by two withdrawn LS coaches, thereby keeping the JCY's in approximate age sequence with Thames Valley's), and entered service without any modification to their single aperture destination boxes, or even a repaint (they were already in red livery).

Four more KSWs were acquired at the end of 1967. These, with AVW engines and L55R bodies, were formerly United Automobile's Nos. BBL66-8/74 (PHN 828/9/1/19) and became Thames Valley's Nos. 688-91. Despite already being red, they received a full repaint this time.

Withdrawals began in 1968 and continued until 1971. Three machines remained in the fleet as driver trainers (Nos. 733/45/8), and when the Thames Valley & Aldershot Omnibus Co. Ltd. (Alder Valley) was formed in 1972, these buses became Nos. 27-29. However, all three were withdrawn from use by late 1974.

*Plate 115:* Thames Valley is famous for operating coach-seated double deckers on its services into London, the practice still being maintained today by Alder Valley. Among Thames Valley's fleet of such vehicles were fifteen KSs and KSWs, which had a seating capacity of 53. The upper deck carried 27 passengers, as found in a normal lowbridge bus, but the lower deck capacity was 26, two fewer than the bus, as the seat spacing caused a reduction to be made to the inward-facing wheel arch seats, from four to three passengers. This can be seen in this interior view of KSW No. 637 (GJB 275), the picture also showing the semi-enclosed luggage rack on the nearside of the ceiling, to 'balance' the intrusion of the sunken offside gangway (this luggage rack was only featured in KSWs of two other fleets — ten buses with Bristol and nine with Southern Vectis). The fifteen coaches were the only KS/KSW family vehicles with Thames Valley to have the benefit of platform doors.

*Courtesy ECW*

*Plate 116:* Thames Valley's six coach-seated KS6Bs, Nos. 595-600 (FMO 977-82) were the only KSs ever to feature platform doors. The combination of enclosed platforms and a panelled nearside quarter bay was unique! With the exception of Brighton, Hove & District's 1957 KSs, these six coaches were the only KSs to have sloping canopies, normally associated with KSWs built with effect from the 1952 order. It is understood that this pattern was necessitated by the type of saloon heating which was installed, the equipment for which was housed above the canopy. Note the lettering for the restrictive 30m.p.h. speed limit, then in force for stage carriage vehicles, and even on limited stop services. No. 598 was photographed by the bodybuilder's official photographer.

*Courtesy ECW*

*Plate 117:* The KSs had the normal three-piece destination layout at the back, but later, Thames Valley was unusual in standardising on T-type boxes at the rear (*see Plate 125*). The KS coaches, together with the KSW versions, were used on the two limited stop routes from Reading to London (Victoria), services A and B, although it was the latter route, via the Great West Road, that was the more frequent and better known (service A ran via Ascot). The bold fleetname of the day is well-portrayed in this official view of No. 598 (FMO 980).

*Courtesy ECW*

*Plate 118:* The first nine Thames Valley KS6Bs were standard buses, although the first three, Nos. 586-8, had the less common oblong registration plate on the cab dash, such as shown in *Plate 69*. No. 593 (FMO 975), seen here, was a Maidenhead-based vehicle, and exemplifies the original condition of the batch. This bus, together with No. 588, later received T-type destination indicators.

*R. F. Mack*

*Plate 119:* No. 603 (FMO 985) was one of Thames Valley's three pre-production KSW6Bs. They were the only examples delivered with oblong registration plates across the foot of the radiator. This bus clearly demonstrates the lack of battery flaps at the bottom of the side panels; Thames Valley was the only company whose KSs and KSWs were not fitted with these hatches. The batteries, instead, were located under the forward part of the lower saloon and were accessible through floor traps. Other companies did have buses with batteries in this position, but their vehicles also had the standard side flaps! Thames Valley was also unusual in fitting five speed gearboxes to its entire KSW fleet. No. 603 is seen at Maidenhead bus station.

*R. H. G. Simpson*

*Plate 120:* The KS coaches, Nos 595-600, had their coach seats cut down (i.e. headrests removed) and reupholstered, during 1964/5, and they were subsequently used on bus duties. The six vehicles were also repanelled, together with the removal of the redundant beading for the upper cream band. They were fitted with T-type destination boxes which, rather strangely, retained the original 48in. wide ultimate site, rather than being changed to the 40in. width that had been standard on new stock since 1955. Whilst on coach duties, all six had been based at Reading, but they were now to be found at other depots. No. 596 (FMO 978), seen at Newbury, shows the later, white, fleet number, placed on the cab dash.

*Michael Bennett*

*Plate 121:* Thames Valley's K family double deckers had the upper cream band discontinued upon repainting, from the end of 1957, yet curiously, LDs continued to be repainted with the upper cream band for a few more years! The revised appearance is illustrated by No. 645 (GJB 283), pictured standing beneath the canopy at Windsor Station. The busy route 2 (Reading to Windsor) was one of the first to be allocated new KSWs of the GJB batch, from the Ascot Depot, and several remained on the route for many years, even after Ascot Depot closed, in 1960, when its allocation was transferred to the new Bracknell Garage.

*R. H. G. Simpson*

*Plate 122:* The intensive network of services between Maidenhead and Slough was operated by vehicles from Maidenhead Depot. This scene at Slough Station shows a good cross-section of that depot's KS/KSW allocation, and three of the afore-mentioned routes. KS6B No. 592 (FMO 974) on route 66, pre-production KSW6B No. 603 (FMO 985) on route 60 and 1951 KSW6B No. 635 (GJB 273) on the 64 route (which ran to Britwell, jointly with London Transport route 400) are joined by 'intruder' LD6B No. 757 (MBL 838), on service 65 for Maidenhead, this Loddeka retaining the upper cream band (*see Plate 121*). It is noteworthy that all three 8ft. wide buses have black steering wheels!

*R. F. Mack*

*Plate 123:* The three 1951 KSW coaches, Nos. 637-9, received the same destination box conversions and repanelling as their KS cousins, as shown in *Plate 120.* No. 637 (GJB 275) had its seats cut down and reupholstered in January 1964, and was one of those to remain at Reading, for bus work. Route 2 (*Plate 121*) was later renumbered into the 90-92 group, and No. 637 is shown near Sunninghill on a variation of the service. The full list of Thames Valley KSWs that received T-type destination boxes is Nos. 601, 637-40/2/4/6/7/50, 695/8, 739/42/6/8.

C. W. Routh

*Plate 124:* Windsor Castle provides an impressive backdrop to a fairly new No. 661 (HBL 63), of 1952. The white-coated policeman, Morris Minor, and London Transport green RT help to complete this period scene. With a running time in excess of two hours, over its full Windsor—High Wycombe—Aylesbury length, service 20 was Thames Valley's longest bus route. No. 661 was allocated to Maidenhead, through which town service 20 passed.

R. F. Mack

*Plate 125:* Most of Thames Valley's KSWs were unusual in being delivered with only the T-type destination display at the back, thereby pre-empting the front conversions to 'T' box, on some of the class, by many years. Thames Valley was another operator to divide the lower rear panels (*see Plates 85 & 94*), as can be seen on No. 656 (HBL 58), standing at Reading Station.

R. F. Mack

*Plate 126:* Maidenhead-based vehicles were fitted with London-style nearside running-number plates, circa 1960; some other depots' buses also received them later, but they were not so widely used as at Maidenhead. No. 667 (HBL 69), seen at Maidenhead bus station in June 1970, employs the stencilled plate. This picture shows the saw-tooth layout of the bus station after rebuilding — the trees and grass bank in the background to *Plate 119* are approximately where the new platforms were made. Judging by the windscreen position of the accompanying LD, No. 784 (NBL 741), the day was rather warm! In the distance can be seen one of the 30 seat SUS4As, acquired from Bristol Omnibus Company.

*Graham Jones*

*Plate 127:* Of all the KS/KSW operators, only Thames Valley and United Automobile Services made widespread use of front-mounted advertisements, alongside the destination boxes, in a position particularly associated with London Transport. No. 697 (HMO 843), one of the 1953 buses, hurries out of Reading, under Corporation trolleybus overhead wires. The rubber/leather strip affixed to the top of the windscreen was a later addition, and more especially associated with examples from a couple of seaside operators, Brighton Hove & District and Weston-super-Mare-based buses of the Bristol Omnibus Company (*see Plate 3*).

*P. J. Relf*

*Plate 128:* Apart from Eastern National's three examples, the only KSWs to run regularly into London were Thames Valley's coaches. The JRX batch, of 1954, lasted well into the 1960s on route B, before replacement by FLF coaches. No. 740 (JRX 815) is seen at Victoria Coach Station in August 1961, in company with Black & White and East Kent coaches.

*Allan Macfarlane*

*Plate 129:* By 1954, Thames Valley was one of only two operators still buying lowbridge KSWs, United Counties being the other. No. 731 (JRX 806) was one of a number of KSWs associated for many years with High Wycombe Depot. This bus illustrates the red masking applied to the front intermediate blind box on several vehicles, yet some Newbury buses actually managed to retain three-line 'via' blinds until withdrawal. No. 731 is seen in Oxford Street, High Wycombe, in June 1969, displaying a particularly uninformative ultimate destination!

*Graham Jones*

*Plate 130:* No. 742 (JRX 817) was one of the four JRX coaches to have the seats cut down. Although receiving a front 'T' box conversion, this was one of several KSWs to have the existing panel modified, rather than completely replaced. The route number tracks have been moved to a central position, the original ultimate screen has been retained, and the surplus sections have been overpanelled. The bus also retains its upper cream band beading. No. 742 is seen at Reading bus station on 4th June 1970, alongside No. D5 (ABL 117B), a coach-seated FLF6B, which itself was in bus livery by this time.

*Graham Jones*

*Plate 131:* This very fortunate photograph captures two of Thames Valley's second-hand KSWs. The six buses acquired from United Welsh at the end of 1966, or a year later from United Automobile, were attached to Newbury Depot for their entire Thames Valley lives. Two of them, No. 691 (PHN 819), formerly United No. BBL74, and No. 673 (JCY 990), previously United Welsh No. 1243, are shown together at the rustic Wharf bus station (now, sadly, superseded) on 4th June 1970, by which time these buses were largely confined to town services or rush hour work. The LS5G alongside was also second-hand, being ex-Bristol Omnibus Company PHW 930.

*Graham Jones*

The KSW fleet of the United Automobile Services Ltd. will be better remembered for its highbridge buses than the lowbridge versions, but the very existence of highbridge buses with United was interesting, as such vehicles were unknown there until the fulfilment of the 1950 order. This order called for fifteen buses which broke the tradition of having lowbridge bodies. Also unusual was the fact that three chassis types made up the order — K6Bs, KS6Bs and KSW6Bs. They were numbered in a new series from BBH1 (i.e. Bristol chassis, Bristol engine, Highbridge bodywork), and registered NHN 901 onwards. The nine Ks and three KSs were intermingled, so that the KSs received fleet numbers BBH7, 11 and 12. Following these, to complete the order, were three pre-production KSWs. For these, the fleet numbers 'skipped' to BBH20-22 (NHN 913-5), probably to draw attention to their extra width.

No double deckers were ordered for 1951, but in 1952 twenty five KSWs were ordered. These increased the variety even more, falling into three classes. Firstly there were five more KSW6B/H6OR buses Nos. BBH23-7 (PHN 805-9), then there were five lowbridge KSW6Bs, Nos. BBL63-67 (PHN 825-9), and finally fifteen lowbridge KSW5Gs, Nos. BGL67-81 (PHN 810-24). (NB: each class series began at 1, hence the apparent duplication of No. 67)

The highbridge KSW had made its mark with United, and no more lowbridge buses appeared. Variety continued, however, as the 1953 order showed. Nos. BBH28-36 (SHN 701-9) were more KSW6Bs, but Nos. BBH28-32 had platform doors. The other six buses of this year's order started yet another class, Nos. BGH1-6 (SHN 710-5). These were KSW5Gs with H6OR bodies, that on No. BGH6 having platform doors.

Again for 1954, fifteen KSWs were ordered (the KSW being preferred to the Lodekka here), but all these were of KSW6B/H6OR layout. They were numbered BBH37-51, with matched registrations UHN 637-44 and VHN 845-51. A supplementary order for another five identical buses materialised as Nos. BBH 52-6 (WHN 52-6) immediately afterwards, only then, in 1955, to be followed by Lodekkas.

Three KSs and 63 KSWs had been delivered, and all were in standard Tilling red livery, with normal three-piece destination boxes.

Commencing in 1959, United embarked on a programme of engine exchange, which resulted in better utilisation of AVW and 5LW units. Consequently, KSW5Gs swapped engines with L6Bs, resulting in the bigger engines being used in the double deckers, and the smaller units in the single deckers. The first exchange took place in April 1959, and involved No. BGH6, which now became a KSW6B, and so was renumbered to the appropriate class, and became No. BBH57 accordingly. This conversion was followed, in this order, by Nos. BGH5, 4, and 3, which became Nos. BBH58-60. Then in November 1959, No. BGL78 became No. BBL68, and during 1960/1, all remaining KSW5Gs were converted to KSW6B, viz: Nos. BGH1 and 2 to BBH61/2, and Nos. BGL75/70/79/67/80/76/77/69/68/73/71/72/74/81 to BBL69-82.

In 1964, as the United Automobile fleet had become practically all-Bristol, the 'B' prefix letter, to indicate Bristol chassis, was dropped, the BBH class becoming BH, for example. However, to avoid confusion with Lodekkas, which until then had carried class letters BL, the lowbridge KSWs remained unchanged as BBL.

Another, more extensive renumbering took place on 1st January 1969, whereby the whole fleet was renumbered into a purely numerical system. The K class Bristols, irrespective of chassis or body type, commenced at No. 51. By now, many withdrawals had been made. They started in a very random order in 1967, and this random order was highlighted by the 1969 renumbering. Nos. 51-4 were K6Bs NHN 901/6/9/10, still giving yeoman service; Nos. 55/6 were KS6B, formerly Nos. BH11/2; then Nos. 57-80 were highbridge KSW6Bs, formerly Nos. BH20/4/8-31/3-5/7/42/6/7/50/3-62. The two remaining lowbridge KSWs, Nos. BBL73/8, became Nos. 81/2.

Five days later, the United operations in Carlisle were transferred, by the National Bus Company, to Ribble, and the KSWs allocated there, Nos. 64, 65 and 73, were due to be handed over to Ribble. However, Ribble had second thoughts about these three vehicles (regrettably!), and although allocated Ribble numbers 1979-81, they were left in United hands, and reallocated to other depots, Nos. 65 and 73 being among the final withdrawal of KSW types, made in July 1970.

*Plate 132:* United Automobile Services' Nos. BBH20-22 (NHN 913-5) were among the last of the 25 pre-production KSW6Bs to enter service, doing so in the summer of 1951. Originally fitted with the registration plate at the foot of the radiator, No. BBH21 had received a square, hand-painted plate on the cab dash, by the time it was seen leaving Durham, on the lengthy Newcastle to Darlington service. It also displays the front-mounted advertisements, familiar on United buses.

*R. F. Mack*

*Plate 133:* Only three KSs were operated by United, these being 7ft. 6in. wide highbridge buses — a fairly uncommon KS variation outside the Bristol fleet. Curiously, the first, NHN 907, was a lone KS which was numbered in the middle of the batch of K6Bs, while the other two, NHN 911/2, followed the last of the Ks. This head-on view of the first of the KSs, by this time numbered BH7, highlights the very narrow effect given by the 7ft. 6in. highbridge version. It was photographed at Bishop Auckland Market Place.

*R. F. Mack*

*Plate 134:* United's first KSW, No. BBH20 (NHN 913), is seen in its original condition, displaying the larger, underlined style of fleetname. It is a good example of an early highbridge KSW, with horizontal nearside canopy and unglazed lower-deck quarter panel. The combination of the radiator-mounted registration plate, and the complete lack of numbering or lettering on the cab dash looks a little odd. One of United's huge fleet of LS5G saloons, No. BU47 (SHN 737), stands behind the KSW.

*Graham Jones Collection*

*Plate 135:* The first two highbridge PHN-registered KSWs, of 1952, were used for many years on Scarborough town services. No. BBH24 (PHN 806) stands amidst architecture typical of this fashionable spa town. United's KSWs were unusual in being delivered with the driver's offside mirror mounted low down on the windscreen pillar. The silver-painted radiator grille, reminiscent of Eastern National practice, was, however, a later addition, and was not perpetuated for any length of time.

*R. F. Mack*

*Plate 136:* This early photograph of PHN 823 as a KSW5G, numbered BGL80, clearly shows the original bold style of fleet numbers used; they were affixed just behind the front wheel. The bus was re-engined with a Bristol AVW unit in October 1960, and was henceforth numbered BBL73. It survived long enough to be one of only two lowbridge KSWs renumbered under the January 1969 scheme, when it became No. 81, although it was withdrawn within a few months. Interestingly, a long-standing United practice was the duplication of service numbers within their area; there was one set for Northumberland and Carlisle regions and one set for County Durham and Yorkshire services! No. BGL80 is pictured on the Darlington-based service 30, whilst KSWs could also be found on Carlisle city route 30.

*R. F. Mack*

*Plate 137:* Another KSW5G, re-engined with a Bristol AVW motor, was PHN 820, which was dealt with in December 1960 and renumbered from No. BGL77 to BBL75. In order to carry fleet numbers on the cab dash from 1962, all United's KSs and KSWs had new oblong front registration plates made, which overlapped the beading above the sidelight, and rather spoilt the appearance. No. BBL75 is seen at Durham bus station in July 1964.

*Allan Macfarlane*

*Plate 138:* In addition to Bristol and Lincolnshire, the only other highbridge KSWs with platform doors were the six examples with United — but these were the only ones in red livery! They were initially used on United's longer double-deck routes, such as Newcastle to Darlington or Newcastle to Middlesbrough, but, in this view, No. BBH30 (SHN 703) has arrived in Darlington on the shorter service 22, during 1959. This bus subsequently saw service with Yorkshire Woollen District (*see Plate 141*).

*Geoff. Stainthorpe*

*Plate 139:* Due to the random withdrawals which affected all batches and ages of KSs and KSWs, a complete cross-section received new numbers under the January 1969 scheme. Two of the three KS6Bs received new numbers and this view of No. 56 (NHN 912), alongside 1953 KSW6B No. 63 (SHN 706), provides a good comparison of the two widths. Interestingly, the KS has received flashing trafficators, while the KSW was never so fitted. Both are seen at Ashington depot. The Northumberland services had been renumbered in the 300 and 400 series some years previously. Both buses carry the later, even-sized capitals style of fleetname on the sides.

*R. F. Mack*

*Plate 140:* Although Newcastle upon Tyne was one of the main centres of United operations, the allocation of KSWs to the city was fairly small. No. BBH41 (UHN 641), a 1954 bus, is seen heading into the city from Blyth, with a Corporation trolleybus in the background. This KSW later spent some years at Scarborough.

*R. F. Mack*

*Plate 141:* In December 1967, United sold four lowbridge KSW6Bs to Thames Valley, Nos. BBL66-68/74 (*see Plate 131*), but a more remarkable sale was that in October 1969, of six highbridge KSW6Bs, to the former BET subsidiary, Yorkshire Woollen District! The buses concerned were Nos. 61 (SHN 703), 67 (UHN 642), 70 (VHN 850), 72 (WHN 54), 77 and 79 (SHN 713/0). In the Yorkshire Woollen District fleet, these were numbered 167/6/8/9/4/5, respectively, and entered service retaining their United livery (not dissimilar to YWD's shade of red) and stayed up to a year with their new owner. No. 166 (UHN 642) is seen displaying 'Dewsbury' in its masked-down destination screen. This picture illustrates well the peculiar position United chose for the nearside flashing trafficator.

*R. H. G. Simpson*

*Plate 142:* In mid-1961, United discontinued the use of intermediate blinds, choosing instead to show the ultimate destination in the former 'via' box. The top site, henceforth, carried a permanent display of the company's fleetname. As can be seen in this view of No. BH47 (VHN 847) at Durham bus station, the underlined style of fleetname was originally used, but after the company adopted an even-sized capital non-underlined fleetname in 1964, the destination box name was changed to match (*see Plate 139*).

*Denis Strange*

*Plate 143:*  Scarborough sea front services were traditionally run by a fleet of unusual single deckers and one of the last of the breed, a lengthened L5G with new, central entrance, Queen Mary-style bodywork, can be seen in the distance. However, in this distinctly wintery view, No. BH37 (UHN 637) is shown on Royal Albert Drive, employed on the route. Scarborough Castle can be seen on the hilltop.

*R. F. Mack*

*Plate 144:*  Berwick upon Tweed is the northernmost town in England and is actually nearer Edinburgh than it is to Newcastle. Allocated to this outpost of United operations was a small number of highbridge KSWs, for use on the town services. No. BH56 (WHN 56) was the last KSW delivered to United, entering service, with its fellow WHNs, in 1955. It was a regular bus here for many years and is pictured passing through an archway in the town walls.

*R. F. Mack*

# UNITED COUNTIES

United Counties Omnibus Co. Ltd. ultimately operated fifteen KS, four 8ft. wide KS, and sixty eight KSW vehicles, all of which had lowbridge bodies with open platforms. These figures include fourteen examples taken over from Eastern National in 1952.

The 1950 United Counties order consisted entirely of KSs, both with 5LW and AVW engines. Numbered 684-697 (FRP 684-97), the KS5Gs were Nos. 686-93/5-7, while Nos. 684/5/94 were KS6Bs. In 1956, Nos. 684/5 received 5LW engines in place of their AVW units. The last four of the batch, Nos. 694-7, were the eight-footers. In 1951, a clean change was made to KSWs (and to Northampton registrations), the batch being Nos. 698 upwards (CNH 698, etc.). No. 698 itself was a KSW5G, but all subsequent models were to be KSW6Bs.

In 1952, United Counties renumbered its fleet in preperation for the absorption of Eastern National's Midland Area, and CNH 706-18 were first numbered 867-74/94-8. The existing KSs and KSWs were renumbered 830-9/51/40/1/52/9-66 respectively, the gaps being left for ex-Eastern National examples to be inserted in approximate chassis number sequence. The take-over came on 1st May 1952, and five KS5Gs and nine KSW5Gs came into the fleet. They took the numbers 825-9 (KSs, RPU 521/2/5-7) and Nos. 875-83 (KSWs, SHK 511/9/20/4/7, TNO 673/4/7/8. Reference should be made to the Eastern National chapter for further details.

United Counties' 1952 batch was numbered 908-13, which marked a return to Northampton registrations (HBD 644-7/2/3),

and in the same year five KSW5Gs that had been ordered by Eastern National arrived at United Counties, becoming Nos. 917-21 (HNV 733-7). It is noticeable that the practice of leaving gaps was to continue. The 1953 order was for Nos. 928-45 (JBD 965-982). The first Lodekkas also arrived with the 1953 order, but for 1954, United Counties called for nine more KSWs. These Nos. 961-9 (KNV 334-42), were among the last lowbridge KSWs built, sharing that distinction with Thames Valley's JRX batch.

An interesting point of detail is that United Counties specifically asked that the draught-excluding glasses on the trailing end of the sliding ventilators be excluded on the 1951 (CNH) batch, whereas this feature was not dropped by ECW generally until the 1954 vehicles. United Counties KSWs were standard vehicles in respect of destination boxes, seats, etc, (the JBDs and KNVs having staggered upper-deck seating) and bore the green livery. The upper cream band was excluded from repaints from the mid-1960s.

Withdrawals took place steadily from 1967 until mid-1973, by which time United Counties was among the last half-dozen companies to run KSWs in passenger service. Four were given an afterlife as trainers, after withdrawal in 1973; Nos. 964/11/33/4 were numbered 13-16, had the offside bulkhead cut away, were equipped with doors to the lower saloon, and received yellow paintwork to the front and rear ends. They were later renumbered 1013-1016, and were sold in 1976.

*Plate 145:* Biggleswade, an ex-Eastern National depot, only operated small numbers of KSWs, but, for many years, several of United Counties' own KSs were allocated to this depot. One of these, No. 837 (FRP 691), a KS5G, is seen in July 1966 at Waresley, a small village on the borders of Huntingdonshire and Cambridgeshire. Like Hants & Dorset, United Counties employed a system of colour codes on the fleet number plates, to denote depot allocation; the Biggleswade colours on the plates of No. 837 are light blue, with black figures and edges.

*G. R. Mills*

*Plate 146:* RPU 522 was originally Eastern National No. 4112, and was allocated to Luton at the time of the take-over by United Counties. Some years later, the bus, now numbered 826, is seen at Kingsbury Square, Aylesbury (in company with a green London Transport roofbox RT), when working a town service. By this time, United Counties had substituted 'via' points, with the rather uninformative and unnecessary word 'Service'. The five ex-Eastern National KSs were mostly withdrawn before United Counties' own examples; No. 826 being the last to go, in April 1968. However, this bus subsequently became a temporary office at Stamford, until 1970.

*R. F. Mack*

*Plate 147:* Four KSs with 8ft. wide bodies, FRP 694-7, were delivered to United Counties early in 1951, with fleet numbers 694-7, although they were renumbered 851/40/1/52, in chassis number order, a year later. No. 851 (FRP 694) was the first one to be delivered, in February 1951, and was also the only Bristol-engined example of the four. The bus is seen in Northampton, where it spent most of its days although, latterly, it worked at Luton and Bedford.

*R. F. Mack*

*Plate 148:* Although most KSs had been 5LW-engined (indeed, two of the three KS6Bs were re-equipped with 5LWs), only one KSW ordered by United Counties, CNH 698, was so powered. However, the nine KSWs taken over from Eastern National, and the five diverted from them, were also KSW5Gs. No. 859, as CNH 698 had become in 1952, was withdrawn in April 1969, but then had an interesting period of use as a temporary waiting room for coach passengers at Luton Depot, until the summer of 1973. The bus is shown in May 1973 and illustrates the lower-deck perimeter seats, those in the upper deck not being used.

*Allan Macfarlane*

*Plate 149:* Numerically, the first of the KSW5Gs acquired from Eastern National was No. 875 (SHK 511). Although not having silver radiator grilles, United Counties, like Eastern National, did paint the wheels of their buses green, as visible on No. 875. This bus is one of the examples to be transferred away from an ex-Eastern National depot, and is seen, in October 1964, in Horseshoe Street, Northampton. The initials on the wall are prophetic about a major holding company which was to enter United Counties' life five years later!

*P. J. Relf*

*Plate 150:* Unusually, the nearside canopy style on United Counties buses changed within the 1951 order, No. 872 (CNH 711), seen here, being one of the last to carry the horizontal canopy. This bus was delivered in April 1952. CNH 713, however, delivered a month later, had the sloping style. Unfortunately, a photograph of CNH 712 has yet to be traced, as this book goes to press. No.872 was associated with Rushden Depot for virtually its whole life, and is seen in the town's High Street in August 1970. This vehicle has been repanelled and now has no battery flaps on the side, giving it the appearance of a Thames Valley bus. Note the black masking to the intermediate destination screen, and also the lack of glass 'flaps' on the trailing ends of the ventilators.

*C. W. Routh*

*Plate 151:* Luton traditionally had the largest concentration of KSWs of any depot, with over twenty being based there in the heyday. One of the regulars was No. 908 (HBD 644), the first of the 1952 order for KSW6Bs, and it is pictured working a town service. In February 1962, this bus was modified with a 40in. wide front ultimate destination site, the size that had been standard on Lodekkas since 1955. At the same time, a 'T' box was installed at the rear. No. 938 (JBD 975) had been similarly modified in 1961, and the two buses are believed to have been the only KSWs with this particular type of front display.

*R. F. Mack*

*Plate 152:* No. 883 (TNO 678) was one of the former Eastern National KSW5Gs that remained in their old territory, and is seen at Bedford bus station, late in life. It is accompanied by FS6B No. 604 (WBD 604) and another ex-Eastern National KSW, No. 876 (SHK 519). This picture shows the very small running number plate, placed above the nearside sidelight on the bulkhead, a feature of Bedford's buses. A 40in. ultimate linen has been installed in this bus.

*T. M. Smith*

*Plate 153:* Although this was one of five KSW5Gs ordered by Eastern National, but delivered to United Counties after the take-over of the Luton and Bedford regions, No. 919 (HNV 735) was placed at the other end of the system, at Kettering — one of United Counties' northernmost depots. The bus is seen operating a town service and illustrates the small, underlined, fleetname, used during the 1950s. Although ordered by Eastern National, note that there are no trailing glasses to the sliding ventilators.

*R. H. G. Simpson*

*Plate 154:* Eight United Counties KSWs (five JBDs and three KNVs) survived to operate into 1973. Seven were withdrawn at the end of May and this one, No. 945 (JBD 982), is seen at Luton on its very last day of service, 31st May. It was one of three active there on that day (Nos. 928/45/69) and is pictured on a service which had a long KSW tradition. This day completed nineteen years of operation for this bus (it was licensed in February 1954), but it was later exported to Canada. The last KSW to remain in service with United Counties was No. 969 (KNV 342), appropriately the last to have been delivered to them, and that bus was retired at the end of June 1973.

*Allan Macfarlane*

*Plate 155:* Several of the 1972/3 KSW withdrawals were quickly purchased by Omnibus Promotions, at a time when lowbridge, half-cab double deckers were eagerly sought after, for export to North American tourist areas. United Counties' Nos. 928/30/45 went to the Toronto Transit Commission in Canada, while others went to the USA. Nos. 929/40 (JBD 966/77) are seen at Omnibus Promotions' premises at Hedingham, Essex, in September 1973, freshly repainted in the inevitable London Transport red livery, and carrying extra marker lights on their front domes.

*G. R. Mills*

*Plate 156:* The KNV series entered service after United Counties' first batch of Lodekkas. Nos. 961/4 were new in September 1954, whilst Nos. 962/3/5-9 took up duty in October, thereby making them among the last lowbridge KSWs to enter service. Being late 1954 models, they had glazed rear registration plates, two tail lights, etc., but, unusually, the offside quarter bay was recessed. In this picture, No. 962 (KNV 335), a Northampton-based vehicle, is seen at Daventry, Market Square, in March 1961, pulling away from a typical United Counties dual-purpose LS.

*C. W. Routh*

# UNITED WELSH

The smallest fleet of KSWs, by a very long way, was that of United Welsh Services Ltd., who ran only four examples of the model. The company had been part of the Red & White empire, but following the sale of that group to the BTC in 1950, United Welsh became a self-standing entity under BTC control. Consequently, Bristols came into the fleet for the first time, and the initial examples, which arrived in 1952, were a pair of highbridge KSW6Gs, numbered 1202/3 (HWN 338/9). These buses had the additional distinction of being the first 6LW-engined KSWs to be built (chassis numbers 92.001/2). Unusually for 1952 buses, these vehicles had the lower-backed style of seat.

United Welsh's fleet contained a large number of highbridge buses, so it was somewhat surprising that orders for 1953 should call for two lowbridge KSWs. This was even more surprising in view of the fact that four Lodekkas were ordered for delivery at the same time. The lowbridge buses, again KSW6G models, duly became Nos. 1242/3 (JCY 989/90), and their arrival brought the United Welsh KSW fleet to its maximum.

The four buses carried the standard Tilling red livery, but they had United Welsh's own style of single aperture destination box — this being fitted at the front only.

The two highbridge buses were withdrawn as early as 1965, and No. 1203 was immediately cut down to form breakdown tender No. W3. No. 1202 was purchased by Edwards of Lydbrook, and was promptly scrapped.

The lowbridge pair was withdrawn towards the end of 1966, but had a happier fate in being sold to Thames Valley for further service (q.v.).

The operating territory of United Welsh and that of its BET neighbour, South Wales Transport, very much overlapped. Once both companies had come under the wing of the NBC this was rationalised, and all local NBC interests were absorbed within an enlarged South Wales Transport. Late in 1974, this company made news by buying a second-hand KSW5G! The bus was one of Eastern National's open-top conversions, WNO 484 (ex-No. 2386). It had been withdrawn the previous year, following an accident, but South Wales Transport repaired it, repainted it poppy red, and placed it in service at Swansea, numbered 500, in the summer of 1975.

*Plate 157:* This rear view of United Welsh No. 1202 (HWN 338) illustrates just what a difference was made to the ECW bodywork by the total lack of rear destination equipment! This legacy from the old Red & White group was to change on later United Welsh Lodekkas (although Red & White's own Lodekkas were never fitted with rear screens). The nearside battery hatches on the four United Welsh KSWs were also non-standard, and the single hatch, seen on No. 1202, can be compared with the standard two flaps as carried by United Automobile Services No. BBL66 (*see Introduction page*).

*Courtesy ECW*

*Plate 158:* No. 1203 (HWN 339), the other bus of United Welsh's highbridge pair of KSW6Gs, shows the distinctive single-piece destination box, of the size used by members of the Red & White group for several years. Although reminiscent of the Bristol Tramways box of the time (*see Plate 23*), its dimensions were slightly smaller. After a service life of only twelve years, this KSW was withdrawn at the end of 1964, for conversion to a towing vehicle. In happier days, No. 1203 arrives in Swansea on one of the services from the Gower Peninsula.

*R. H. G. Simpson*

*Plate 159:* The pair of lowbridge United Welsh KSW6Gs entered service in the summer of 1953, a year after the highbridge buses. They were a familiar sight for many years around Neath, where No. 1242 (JCY 989) is seen. This bus later suffered accident damage in United Welsh's service, and was repaired with slightly squarer cab dash beading, etc., as can be seen in *Plate 161*. Lowbridge KSW6Gs only occurred in three fleets — United Welsh (two buses), Bristol (five) and West Yorkshire (ten), which totted up to only seventeen specimens, and those with United Welsh were the only ones with open platforms.

*R. H. G. Simpson*

*Plate 160:* Highbridge KSW No. 1203 (HWN 339), shown in *Plate 158*, appeared completely rebuilt as breakdown tender No. W3, in early 1965. Apart from West Yorkshire KSW6G LWR 424, it was the only KSW to be so converted. Painted in a dark blue livery, No. W3 was based at Neath. The vehicle passed to South Wales Transport upon the amalgamation of the local NBC subsidiaries, on 1st January 1971, and was renumbered 4. It was withdrawn in 1974, but provided spares for the rebuilding of the damaged open-top KSW, WNO 484. The remains of the towing vehicle were finally sold for breaking in 1979.

*R. F. Mack*

*Plate 161:* In 1966, the two lowbridge KSW6Gs passed to Thames Valley, although, surprisingly, they were re-engined with Bristol AVW motors before entering service at Newbury. However, this June 1970 view of No. 672 (JCY 989), shows the bus retaining the bonnet side suited to Gardner engines (i.e. both access holes are on the same level). The vehicle is seen at Newbury bus station, amidst a marvellous cross-section of the Thames Valley fleet — another KSW, LSs, LDs, an FLF, and an RESL — and included is another former United Welsh bus, LD No. 796 (NCY 635), which stands closest to JCY 989. Both ex-United Welsh KSWs were withdrawn by Thames Valley later in 1970, but even then they were to remain together, in the fleet of Riverside Coaches of Harlow, Essex.

*Graham Jones*

*Plate 162:* In the summer of 1975, South Wales Transport placed into service their No. 500 (WNO 484), a 1953 KSW5G, to inaugurate a new open-top coastal service from Swansea city centre, round the edge of Swansea Bay and through Oystermouth to Limeslade, on The Mumbles. The bus is seen at Limeslade beach on 24th August 1976, looking particularly smart after its rebuild and overhaul (during which the registration plate was placed on the radiator). As a source of spares, South Wales Transport acquired two further KSWs in the mid-1970s, both from Bristol, namely OHY 934 and WHW 816.

*Graham Jones*

*Plate 163:* In 1977, No. 500 (WNO 484) was surprisingly repainted silver, as part of the celebrations to mark the Silver Jubilee of Her Majesty Queen Elizabeth II. This was the first year in which bi-lingual fleetnames appeared on SWT buses, the Welsh version, 'De Cymru', appearing on the offside, as shown by this July 1977 view. No. 500 was returned to red livery in 1978 and, despite being joined by three new convertible open-top VRs that summer, the KSW continued in service. The year 1983 was expected to be No. 500's last season, but happily, this 31-year-old KSW5G emerged, in the summer of 1984, resplendent in a new white livery, with red waistband, bonnet and wings, and *Skyrider* names.

*G. R. Mills*

# WEST YORKSHIRE

The sixty-strong West Yorkshire Road Car Co. Ltd. fleet of KSs and KSWs could be broken down into two distinct parts — the main fleet that ran lowbridge buses, and the York-West Yorkshire subsidiary that ran highbridge 7ft. 6in. buses in the narrow streets of York.

Ten lowbridge buses were ordered for 1950. Six materialised as KS6Bs, numbered 804/5/10-3 (JWY 222/3/8-31), while the other four were pre-production KSW6Bs, Nos. 806-9 (JWY 224-7).

West Yorkshire was one of only two operators to order KSs in the 1951 programme (Southern Vectis was the other). The eight KS6Bs received had highbridge bodies, and were for the York city fleet, being numbered Y814-Y821 (KWU 353-60). A further two were later added to the order, and became Nos. Y843/4 (KWU 396/7), and entered service in 1952.

The rest of the 1951 order comprised twenty lowbridge KSW6Bs for the main fleet, Nos. 823-842 (KWU 361-80). No. 822, incidentally, was the second prototype Lodekka (JWT 712). Twenty more lowbridge KSWs, but this time with platform doors, were ordered for 1952. The first ten, Nos. 845-54 (LWR 411-20) were again KSW6Bs, but Nos. 855-64 (LWR 421-30) were on KSW6G chassis.

Soon after delivery, Nos. 851 was subjected to a most interesting reconstruction. It was rebuilt to a 51 seat coach (CL27/24RD) with non-opening side windows, a special ventilation system, and built-up front wings. Side-by-side destination boxes were fitted, and the flamboyant design was completed by extensive chrome brightwork to the black livery. The vehicle subsequently received minor detail modifications, and several variations of the red bus livery.

In 1954, West Yorkshire embarked on a fleet renumbering scheme, using the prefix letter system and each class commencing at 1. On the KSs and KSWs, the first letter described the vehicle ('D' for double decker) while the second letter indicated the engine make ('B' for Bristol, 'G' for Gardner). Additionally, KSWs had a third letter, 'W', to signify 'Wide', while York's buses still retained the 'Y' prefix. Under this scheme, the lowbridge KSs, Nos. 804/5/10-3 became Nos. DB58-63, York's highbridge KSs Nos. Y814-21/43/4 became Nos. YDB82-91, the KSW6Bs Nos. 806-9/23-42/5-54 were renumbered DBW1-34, and the KSW6Gs were renumbered from 855-64 to DGW1-10.

During 1954/5, Nos. DBW5-24 (the KWUs) were fitted with platform doors and also in 1955, eleven pre-war K5Gs were extensively reconstructed. Their bodies were scrapped, the chassis rebuilt, and given new numbers 12701-11, and new 'short' KS-type bodies were built for them. They were, in essence, new vehicles, so besides receiving new fleet numbers YDG82-92, they were also reregistered OWT 195-205. The highbridge bodies seated only 55 or 56 passengers (H29/26R or H28/28R).

All West Yorkshire group buses were built to standard specification, and carried the red livery. Staggered seating was experimentally fitted to No. 830 in 1952, this layout having been designed by West Yorkshire and even patented by them. Subsequently, during 1955/6, staggered seating was also installed in Nos. DBW1/9/13-6/9/23/4. Nos. 853-64 had been delivered with staggered seating.

Withdrawals of the lowbridge KSs took place during 1965/6. KSW withdrawals started in 1966 (except that No. DBW31, the coach, went in 1964) and all had gone by 1969. Only then did the York city highbridge KSs come off the road — No. YDB90 went early in 1969, but the rest stayed until 1970.

The reconstructed K5Gs, Nos. YDG82-92, were also withdrawn during 1969/70, and YDG83/4/8/92 joined six ex-United KSW6Bs in service with the former BET operator, Yorkshire Woollen District. They became Nos. 155/4/2/3 in that fleet, and were only initially on loan. No. YDG91 replaced No. YDG84 as No. 154 after one month. They were purchased by Yorkshire Woollen District in August 1969. Retaining their West Yorkshire red livery, they were withdrawn by the Dewsbury company during 1970.

After withdrawal in 1969, No. DGW4 was cut down to form a recovery vehicle, and was renumbered 4044. It was the only KSW to be retained by West Yorkshire for further use, but was withdrawn in 1978.

*Plate 164:* Although Eastern Counties had the greatest number of variations of KSs, only West Yorkshire and its associated fleets owned both lowbridge and highbridge KSs built to the normal 7ft. 6in. width. No. DB61 (JWY 229) was new in November 1950 as No. 811, and is shown in this magnificent period scene from the second half of the 1950s, entering Leeds, with Corporation trams in evidence ( the system did not close until 1959), together with two of the most popular Austin and Morris cars of the period. Although the 'via' blind on this KS6B displays the word 'service' in this view, three-line intermediate blinds continued to be used well into the 1960s by West Yorkshire.

R. F. Mack

*Plate 165:* No. DBW4 (JWY 227) was one of the four pre-production KSW6Bs which entered service on 1st January 1951. These buses, as so often had been the case, originally had oblong registration plates mounted at the foot of the radiator. The plates were later moved to the cab dash, but overlapped the beading, in the same way that was later found in United Automobile's fleet. Sister bus No. 808 (DBW3) was new with a five-speed gearbox, as were a couple of Bristol Tramways' pre-production KSWs.

*R. F. Mack*

*Plate 166:* Apart from Southern Vectis, the only operator to take KSs in 1952 was West Yorkshire. KWU 357 was new as No. Y818 in January 1952, although, in this picture, the bus carries the fleet number YDB86. These ten highbridge KS6Bs were specifically required for the York-West Yorkshire fleet, whose services negotiated some very narrow streets within that city. Concurrently, the main West Yorkshire fleet was placing lowbridge KSWs in service.

*R. F. Mack*

*Plate 167:* York's No. YDB83 (KWU 354) is shown, in its final condition, approaching the railway station on 18th August 1967. This bus, together with Nos. YDB87 and YDB91, received T-type destinations in 1963 (at least Nos. DBW24 and DGW2 also gained 'T' boxes). It will be seen that a mask containing the new arrangement, which includes the narrower 40in. ultimate site, has been placed over the original screens. The bus also carries the even-sized block capital style of fleetname, which first appeared around 1960. No. YDB83 and twin No. YDB84 were the last two KSs to be withdrawn, in November 1970, and were also the last buses of the K family to remain in service with the West Yorkshire fleets! Regrettably, none of these KSs saw further service after sale. Note the glazed quarter bay, alongside the platform — an uncommon feature on KS bodywork.

*P. J. Relf*

*Plate 168:*  West Yorkshire No. 823 (KWU 361) was the first of the 1951 order for twenty lowbridge KSW6Bs, and entered service in November of that year. It will be seen that, unusually, these buses had sloping canopies, being the first vehicles, apart from Thames Valley's coaches, to have this feature. The platform doors were a later addition, however, and were fitted around 1954/5. In this respect they were interesting, too, as they were the only KSWs of any fleet to be modified in this way. West Yorkshire's KSs and KSWs were subjected to the silver radiator grille treatment (*see Plates 135 & 136 and the Eastern National section*), until 1956, after which time they were changed to black upon repainting. No. DBW5, to give the bus its post-1954 fleet number, leaves Harrogate for Bradford, amidst period street furnishings.

*R. F. Mack*

*Plate 169:*  Delivered as a normal member of the 1952 KSW6B order, towards the end of that year, West Yorkshire's No. 851 (LWR 417) was taken straight into the company's workshops and rebuilt to a flamboyant and unique 51 seater coach! It was outshopped in 1953 in a dramatic 'Coronation' livery of black, with extensive areas of chrome trim. All nearside lower-saloon seats faced forward, including those over the wheel arch and, for the benefit of passengers in the latter seats, the adjacent window was raised above the line of the others. The offside wheel arch seat was inward-facing, as normal, and in any case, the intrusion of the upper-deck gangway prevented the offside window from being raised. Also visible in this view are the transparent amber panels inserted into the centre of the roof and front dome. The round intakes, either side of the 'side-by-side' front destination box, admitted air to both decks (assisted by fans) and, for this reason, all sliding ventilators were removed. The air from the saloons was expelled through the cove panels (note the trunking along the edge of the roof) or through louvres above the downstairs windows. The rather ungainly built-up front wings are evident in this view of No. 851, which, despite its fascinating appearance, is hardly the most attractive KSW to grace our roads!

*R. F. Mack*

*Plate 170:* This offisde rear view of West Yorkshire's coach, No. 851, shows several interesting features. Firstly, it will be seen that the rear destination equipment was removed, and that the offside window line was not altered (the longitudinal seat can be seen). Most interestingly, the rear emergency exit and adjacent windows have been raised, as have the windows in the platform doors (*see also Plate 169*). Additional luggage space was provided under the staircase and to gain access, a hatch was built into the rear panel; this hatch encompassed the registration plate. A special script form of the fleetname adorned the side panels. No. 851, seen in this view, wearing trade plates, entered service in May 1953 at Bradford Depot, principally for use on the Bradford to Scarborough service.

*R. F. Mack*

*Plate 171:* In 1954, the KSW coach was repainted red and cream, whilst retaining all of the chrome brightwork. Probably as a result of opinions expressed by drivers, the bulbous built-up nearside front wing was removed, and replaced by a standard wing, both wings, it will be noticed, being painted red. The two translucent amber panels in the front dome can be seen more clearly in this picture. Allocated to York for much of its later life, the coach, numbered DBW31 since 1954, is seen turning out of Rougier Street, with York Minster forming the backdrop.

*R. F. Mack*

*Plate 172:* Following the removal of the built-up nearside front wing, the next change to overcome West Yorkshire's unique KSW coach now saw the replacement of the built-up offside front wing by a standard unit! At the same time, the cab dash was restored to its original design, complete with square registration plate. A further revision of the livery saw the elimination of the chrome trim, by the application of cream paint to the waistband and red paint elsewhere. The window surrounds remained cream, but the wings now became black. In this view of No. DBW31 in this condition, the bus is facing directly towards Rougier Street, York, and the scene of *Plate 171*.

*R. F. Mack*

*Plate 173:* The last livery style of No. DBW31 represented something approaching standard bus livery, although the upper cream band was thicker, due to the lack of suitable beading. However, in this scheme, the lower cream band now followed the stepped line of the beading around the staircase panel. The KSW coach (or bus!) is seen standing at York Station, with SGW8 (JYG 723), an LL5G with 8ft. wide bodywork, the single deck contemporary of the 8ft. KS. No. DBW31 was withdrawn in September 1964 and thus gained the dubious distinction of becoming the first scheduled KSW withdrawal in the country! So ended the fascinating career of the most novel vehicle, as far as West Yorkshire was concerned, but happily, LWR 417 was to see further use, albeit for only four more years, with Regent Bingo of Batley, Yorks.

*R. F. Mack*

*Plate 174:* The last KSW to enter service with West Yorkshire was No. DGW10 (LWR 430), which took up duty on 1st July 1953. It was also one of the last KSWs to be withdrawn by the company, in February 1969. This Gardner 6LW-engined bus had a five speed gearbox, platform doors, and staggered seating on the upper deck — quite clearly visible in this picture. The idea of placing the seats in a staggered fashion, instead of straight across, emanated from West Yorkshire, in 1952, and the arrangement was subsequently adopted as standard by ECW, for the later lowbridge bodies (*see Plate 205 for interior view*). Although most depots operated KS/KSW buses, Leeds and Bradford had by far the largest allocations. West Yorkshire had some of the longest KSW routes in the country, as routes 43, Leeds to Scarborough, and 44, Leeds to Bridlington, were both over sixty miles in length and regularly employed KSWs during the 1950s. No. DGW10, a rare example of the lowbridge KSW6G combination (*see Plate 159*) stands outside Leeds Depot, with its blinds set for a short working of the 43 service to York.

*R. F. Mack*

*Plate 175:* In 1955, eleven pre-war K5G chassis emerged from a very extensive refurbishing programme, bearing brand-new 'short' KS style bodies. The 1939 chassis had very few of the original components remaining, having been given new frames, radiators, etc., while all running units had been thoroughly overhauled. They even gained new chassis numbers, 12701-11, (a style of numbering that did not fit into Bristol's system) and were therefore obliged to be given new registrations, OWT 195-205. The 7ft. 6in. wide bodywork, for some reason, did not carry the normal 60 seats of the KS. Strangely, some vehicles had 56 seats (Nos. YDG82/4/8/9), while the others, Nos. YDG83/5-7/90-2, had an even lower capacity, of only 55! Newly delivered, a gleaming No. YDG89 (OWT 202) carries a fleet number in the short-lived position, below the first side window.

*R. F. Mack*

*Plate 176:* As on the six rebodied Brighton, Hove & District Ks (*Plates 12 & 13*), York-West Yorkshire's 1955 OWT-registered reconstructed K5Gs had KSW-style beading on the cab dash, together with a deeper windscreen, as clearly detectable in this photograph of No. YDG85 (OWT 198), one of the 55 seaters. Another curious feature was that they retained the Autovac method of oil feed, unlike the far less extensively modified Ks of Brighton, Hove & District and Hants & Dorset, which received similar bodies (*see also Plates 95 & 96*). The appearance of the Autovac tank on the bulkhead of the KS-style body looked grossly inept! No. YDG85 passes through the city walls of York at Walmgate Bar, with little headroom to spare (a good enough reason to specify 7ft. 6in. bodywork!), as it heads out of the city. All this batch remained intact until 1969.

*R. F. Mack*

# WESTERN NATIONAL
# SOUTHERN NATIONAL

If the combined Western National and Southern National fleet of KS/KSW buses is remembered for nothing else, then it certainly will be remembered for the fact that all three batches were registered in one common series — the extensive LTA block, which totalled a grand 277 registrations, covering all types of Bristol available at the beginning of the 1950s!

There were seventy buses of KS and KSW type and, interestingly, exactly half were of the KS variety. In fact, Southern National was the only operator to have more KSs than KSWs. All examples were lowbridge, and all had open platforms, although Clayton circular heaters were fitted on both decks.

The joint fleets had accumulated very nearly 200 Ks since the war, so K-class Bristols accounted for a large proportion of the fleet for very many years. In fact, the 1950 vehicle order started with Ks, namely Nos. 989-992 (LTA 808-11) K5G/L55R, for the Western National fleet. After these came the first KSs, Nos. 993-999 and No. 1800 (LTA 812-9), KS5Gs. (Western National/Southern National's numbering system at the time employed blocks of 100 or 200 numbers for a particular type, which, when completed, were increased by 1000; e.g. 800-999, followed by 1800, etc.) The next Western National buses were two of the pre-production run of KSW6Bs, and were numbered 1801/2, (LTA 820/1). More KS5Gs followed, Nos 1803-9 (LTA 822-8), and then came three KS6Bs with 8ft. wide bodywork, Nos. 1810-2 (LTA 829-31), plus an 8ft. KS5G, No. 1813 (LTA 832).

Southern National's 1950 batch was basically the same, except that it lacked the Ks. The first three buses of the order, however, were diverted to Western National, to compensate for the diversion of three of their Ks to Southern National during the previous year. These were Nos. 1826-8 (LTA 936-8), KS5Gs. Similar buses, Nos. 1829-31/4/5/7-9 (LTA 939, etc.) followed, for Southern National. Nos. 1832/3 (LTA 942/3) were KSW6Bs of the pre-production run, and No. 1836 (LTA 946) was a lone KS6B. Nos. 1840-3 (LTA 950-3) were 8ft. wide KS5Gs.

The 1951 order for both companies was rather small. Southern National had only four buses, Nos. 1844-7 (LTA 954-7), which were KSW6Bs, and Western National had only a dozen machines, Nos. 1814-25 (LTA 833-44). Of these, Nos. 1814/5/21-5 were also KSW6Bs, but Nos. 1816-20 were KSW5Gs.

For 1952, Southern National received five buses, and Western National ten. All were KSW6Bs, the former being numbered 1848-52 (LTA 991-5), and the latter 1853-62 (LTA 854/5, 879-86). The companies immediately adopted the Lodekka when it became available after 1953, and no more KSWs were delivered.

The buses were to standard specification in most respects, except that the registration plates were carried across the bottom of the radiator in true Western National/Southern National tradition. Staggered upper-deck seating was fitted to Nos. 1851/2/60-2. Tilling green livery was worn by the fleet, and the black lining-out to the cream bands was always maintained, greatly enchancing the appearance. These vehicles were kept in very smart condition, and this paid off by the long life which the company gained from its buses — withdrawals in general did not start until 1969, and a number saw 20 or 21 years of service. However, replacement was swift, and the last ran in 1971. An earlier withdrawal befell No. 1823 in 1963, after severe fire damage at Trowbridge Depot.

*Plate 177:* Many of Western National and Southern National's KSs and KSWs spent their entire lives without moving from a particular depot or region. One such bus was KSW6B No. 1853 (LTA 854), the first of Western National's 1952 order. This bus spent some seventeen years based at Penzance, before moving to nearby Helston to end its days. It is pictured at St. Ives, having reversed to the precarious edge of the elevated bus station, above this congested resort, and is ready to take out a short working of the Penzance route. All these operators' K family buses were characterised by the positioning of the registration plate across the foot of the radiator. The cab dash was then free to carry not only the heavy cast fleet number plate, but also the company's fleetname, these being the only fleets in the BTC, other than Westcliff-on-Sea, to practise this.

*J. H. Aston*

*Plate 178:* There is a certain amount of romance attached to Western National and Southern National's buses, as so many people were introduced to them as a result of spending memorable summer holidays in Dorset, Devon and Cornwall. This scene typifies the companies' operations to a popular beach, generally reached by travelling down steep, narrow lanes — a great deal of stopping and starting and low gear work, often with a full load of chatty holiday-makers, whose words were usually lost below the shrill ring of excited children's voices! Western National's Nos. 993-8 (LTA 812-7) were all allocated to Cornish depots. Nos. 996/7 were based at Camborne, and the former is pictured by the beach at Portreath. This view gives a particularly good impression of the narrowness of the model. In 1964, all six of these KS5Gs were transferred to other areas.

*R. F. Mack*

*Plate 179:* Most KSs that were built, plus all 25 pre-production KSWs and early production KSWs into the 1951 order, were completed with an unglazed panel in the nearside lower-deck quarter bay. Most vehicles retained this throughout their lives, only Bristol Omnibus Company and Hants & Dorset taking the trouble of inserting a glazed panel. Western National No. 1800 (LTA 819), a KS5G seen at Bridgwater in March 1968, exemplifies the unglazed panel and also illustrates the well-known 'Western National Service No.' display in the rear screen — if such a display must be used, this then is a great improvement on the mere 'Service' used by other companies. It will be seen that a miniature version of the fleetname was carried on the back panel, as well as on the cab dash.

*Graham Jones*

*Plate 180:* Inter-fleet transfers between Southern National and Western National were fairly uncommon. They did not affect the KS/KSW family at all during their service lives, excepting the group of buses involved when Southern National's entire operations passed to Western National in November 1969. However, three KS5Gs which had been ordered by Southern National in 1950, entered service with Western National, to make up for three K6Bs which had been 'moved' the opposite way, on delivery, earlier in 1950. The KSs, Nos. 1826-8 (LTA 936-8), were again Cornish buses for many years. No. 1828 is seen at Penzance railway station in August 1961, although it ended its days at Totnes in Devon, sometimes working the services in the Paignton area, 'competing' with BET rival, Devon General. As it happened, Nos. 1826-8 were the longest-lived of all Southern National and Western National KSs, even outliving their 8ft. wide sisters. They were not withdrawn until mid-1971; Hants & Dorset's KSs alone had a slightly longer life (*see Plate 84*).

*P. J. Relf*

*Plate 181:* Although operating numerous Ks, the large depot at Plymouth was never particularly associated with the KSs or KSWs; indeed, no KSWs were ever allocated on a regular basis. However, two KS5Gs, Nos. 1805/7 (LTA 824/6), were based here from new and never moved away from the South Devon area. Later, in the 1960s, sister buses Nos. 996-8 and Nos. 1826/7 all saw service at Plymouth, while, after sale by Western National, No. 995 ran for the Royal Navy on their Devonport Dockyard service. No. 1807 is seen at Saltash Passage, on the Devon side of the River Tamar, standing at the foot of one of the massive stone piers supporting Brunel's Saltash railway bridge, high above the bus. The KS is working one of the Plymouth Joint Services city routes, the 5, 6 and 7 group then, as now, being run entirely by Western National.

*Geoff Stainthorpe*

*Plate 182:* Southern National's KS and KSW fleet was principally found in their Somerset and Dorset area, while the remote North Devon and North Cornwall area saw only a handful of KS5Gs allocated (KSWs were not operated here). For all that, Nos. 1829-31/7 were particularly associated with North Devon. This view of No. 1830 (LTA 940), trundling into Ilfracombe, captures the relaxed and sleepy atmosphere which many North Devon locations seemed to possess, despite the large influx of summer tourists.

*R. F. Mack*

*Plate 183:* While most KSWs in the two fleets were powered by Bristol AVW engines, the majority of KSs had Gardner 5LW units, only four having the larger Bristol motor. However, three of the four 8ft. wide KSs in Western National's ownership were KS6Bs, including No. 1811 (LTA 830), seen standing at Helston, in August 1961, on a route that would have taken it close to the most southerly point on the British mainland, The Lizard. Behind No. 1811 is one of the uncommon Beadle-bodied Bedford OBs, No. 524 (HUO 677), which was withdrawn later that year.

*P. J. Relf*

*Plate 184:* Certain of the longer services were operated jointly by Western National and Southern National. One example was route 264 in Somerset, between Yeovil (a Southern National town) and Taunton (in Western National territory, although, since 1983, it has been within the area of the resurrected Southern National). No. 1832 (LTA 942), awaiting departure from its home town of Yeovil, was one of two pre-production KSW6Bs allocated to Southern National (Western National also had a pair). These were among the first Bristols to be fitted with the familiar white steering wheel, which was adopted by most operators to draw the driver's attention to the fact that he was in control of an 8ft. wide bus. The white wheel contrasts with the black wheel in K5G No. 976 (KUO 989), seen beyond the KSW.

*A. M. Wright*

*Plate 185:* The cast metal fleet number plates were a familiar feature of both fleets, and usually employed a black painted background. However, several Southern National buses had green painted plates, thereby producing a less distinctive effect. No. 1842 (LTA 952), an 8ft. KS5G, was one such example. This well-laden bus is seen at Swanage, in August 1958, ready to depart on the picturesque route through the Isle of Purbeck, to Weymouth, complete with a standing load! Incidentally, the breadth of Southern National and Western National's joint territory, between Swanage and Penzance, was not far short of 200 miles . . . and a lot more if Devon General's territory was circumnavigated!

*P. J. Relf*

*Plate 186:* There were plenty of locations in the south of England where KS and KSWs of various fleets met. One place where this continued on a regular basis until a very late stage was Bridgwater, in Somerset, a town principally served by Western National. Furthermore, it was the southernmost terminus of Bristol Omnibus Company's route from Burnham-on-Sea, which used highbridge KSWs right through until 1971 (*see Plate 43*). On 17th February 1968, Bristol's No. 8181 (SHW 351) arrives at the bus station, whilst Western National No. 1817 (LTA 836) awaits custom on a town service. Both buses are Gardner-engined KSWs, in green livery, but No. 8181 is a highbridge bus with a 6LW power unit, and No. 1817 is a lowbridge bus with a 5LW motor.

*Graham Jones*

*Plate 187:* No. 1825 (LTA 844) represents the 1951 order for KSW6Bs for Western National. The bus looks in original condition when seen at Taunton in March 1969, the only modification being the addition of the flashing trafficators. These buses always retained black lining to the cream bands, although the use of the 'via' point destination blind was becoming rare at that time. Within a year of this photograph being taken, this bus achieved fame by being transferred, together with twin No. 1824, to Bristol Omnibus Company ownership, when the latter operator took over the Western National depot and services at Trowbridge, in Wiltshire (*see Plate 48*).

*Graham Jones*

*Plate 188:* Few of the many depots of the two fleets ever had more than half a dozen KSs and KSWs allocated, at any one time. However, by far the largest total was concentrated at Weymouth, where approximately fifteen Southern National examples were regularly allocated. This view shows 1951 KSW6B No. 1846 (LTA 956) at the King's Statue, on the sea front, in April 1970, at the beginning of its last season in service. By this time, the bus was actually in Western National ownership, having been one of six KSs and nine KSWs to remain with Southern National, upon its absorption by the larger partner, in November 1969. Although the Western National name was carried in the ultimate destination site, it is thought that none of the buses involved ever received a change of fleetname.

*Graham Jones Collection*

*Plate 189:* Southern National had only five KSWs to the 1952 order (identifiable by the sloping canopy) No. 1848 (LTA 991) was the first of the batch and was one of few KSWs to be found at Yeovil, rather than Weymouth. This picture shows the bus at Salisbury, after working the 43 mile service 27 from Yeovil. Not surprisingly, this route, jointly worked with Wilts & Dorset, did not survive the 1950s! Salisbury saw more KSWs from different fleets than any other place in the country, as examples from Southern National, Bath Services, Hants & Dorset and, of course, Wilts & Dorset all regularly ran into the city, during the 1950s. Additionally, there were occasional workings by Western National, from Trowbridge, and by Bristol Tramways.

*R. H. G. Simpson*

# WILTS & DORSET

When asked to give an example of a typical post-war Wilts & Dorset bus, one could very well suggest a red, open-platformed, lowbridge KSW5G. Wilts & Dorset took a large fleet of these, and there were few variations. A total of 8 KSs and 69 KSWs was delivered between 1950 and 1953, in four straightforward batches.

The 1950 order was of a size in keeping with the company's previous post-war deliveries, in calling for eight KSs — five KS6Bs Nos. 314-8 (GMR 893/4, GMW 194-6) and three KS5Gs, Nos. 319/20/4 (GMW 850/1, GWV 305). Double and single-deck vehicles shared a common numbering system up to this point, which resulted in Nos. 321-3 being allocated to LLs. The registrations, it will be noted, were in Wilts & Dorset's well-known 'system' that did not make use of pre-booked blocks. No. 324 differed from the others, in having 8ft. wide bodywork.

Early in the War, as a result of the establishment of a considerable number of military camps in the region of Salisbury Plain, Wilts & Dorset had been obliged to purchased large numbers of extra double deckers. Many were second-hand, and the company was faced with the problem of replacing these worn out and aged vehicles in the early 1950s. For 1951, therefore, no fewer than 34 KSW5Gs were ordered. These became Nos. 325-58 (GWV 929, HAM 229-31, 693-6, HHR 60-4, 750/1, 822/3, HMR 12, 58/9, 414-6, 624, 688-90, 743-7, 809/10). They were followed for 1952 by a further twenty, which were numbered 359-78, with registrations HMW 445-8, HWV 292-4, JAM 419/20, 933, JHR 140-2, 883, 959/60 and JMW 243, 317, 499, 955.

The 1953 batch differed in two respects. Firstly, they had KSW6B chassis, and secondly, their bodies had platform doors.

Fifteen such vehicles were delivered, becoming Nos. 379-93 (JMW 954, JWV 263, 380-3, 849, 978/9, KAM 594/5, KHR 103/4, 529/30), but ten Lodekkas were ordered at the same time, so these were to be the last KSWs for Wilts & Dorset.

Such was the quantity, that the KSWs accounted for about half of Wilts & Dorset's double-fleet. They were of standard specification, with staggered seating being fitted to No. 375 onwards.

Withdrawals started in 1966 (except that Nos. 319 and 339 were scrapped in 1962 and 1965, respectively, after accidents). As a result of merging the management with Hants & Dorset in 1969 (the Wilts & Dorset registered office moved to Bournemouth in 1965), the latter company made steps towards integrating the fleets in 1971, by renumbering both fleets into parallel systems. The surviving Wilts & Dorset KSWs were allocated the series up to No. 399, which would obviously cause some confusion. Thus, 1951 buses, Nos. 329/30/2/42/57, became Nos. 363-7, 1952 examples Nos. 359-70/3/5-8 became Nos. 368-84, and the 1953 batch, Nos. 379-93, became Nos. 385-99. Several of these vehicles had already been withdrawn and did not therefore run with their new numbers.

On 1st October 1972, six KSW5Gs and several of the KSW6Bs were transferred to Hants & Dorset ownership, when Wilts & Dorset was finally absorbed by the larger of the two companies. However, only a handful of these KSWs were to see service with Hants & Dorset and, as the entire 1953 batch of 6Bs had gone by the end of 1972, it was to be the open-platformed KSW5Gs which continued to run, in dwindling numbers, until their final withdrawal in 1974.

*Plate 190:* Four Wilts & Dorset's KS6Bs, Nos. 315-8, were the first new buses allocated to the Basingstoke area of North Hampshire by Wilts & Dorset, after its take-over of Venture Ltd., from the Red & White group, on 1st January 1951. These four buses had been delivered in October and November 1950, but were reserved as Venture stock replacement, and did not enter service until 1st January 1951. They were even licensed to Venture, although they carried Wilts & Dorset fleetnames. It was not until July 1961 that the vehicles' licences were finally transferred from the South Eastern Traffic Area to the Western Traffic Area, at Salisbury. No. 318 (GMW 196) is seen in August 1961 at Basingstoke, on a town service, long before the bus station was built. The crew are attired in the summer version of the once familiar Tilling group uniform.

*G. Mead*

*Plate 191:* All of the earliest Wilts & Dorset KS/KSW buses, between Nos. 314 and 334, were rebuilt by the company with T-type destination boxes, and with 40in. ultimate sites, front and rear. No. 314 (GMR 893) was the first so treated, in March 1961. However, Wilts & Dorset did not bother to replace the small nearside quarter panel with glazing. In this view, No. 314 receives cleaner's and fueler's attention at the end of a busy day at Basingstoke. It is parked in the company of two L6Bs, Nos. 306/8 (GHR 867 and GMR 29), both of which carry the distinctive and unique destination layout, adopted as standard by Wilts & Dorset from 1946 until the arrival, in 1950, of the KSs with their Tilling standard three-piece displays. In January 1962, sister KS, No. 319, had the dubious honour of becoming the first KS or KSW from any fleet, to be withdrawn, after only 12 years' service. Its end, however, was hastened by a serious accident, in Basingstoke.

*R. H. G. Simpson*

*Plate 192:* KS5G No. 324 (GWV 305) remained unique in the Wilts & Dorset fleet, as the only KS to be delivered with an 8ft. wide body. It was also the only bus in their KS/KSW fleet to have an oblong registration plate at the foot of the radiator (apart from the trainers, which were modified at a much later date). Salisbury city services were associated with Lodekkas, right from the delivery of Wilts & Dorset's first batch of LDs, in 1954 and subsequently, KSs and KSWs were not very common on these services. No. 324, however, was an exception, and spent many years so employed. It is pictured in the city centre.

*Michael Bennett*

*Plate 193:* A sizeable proportion of the large 1951 order for KSW5Gs entered service at Salisbury, mainly for use on country routes. No. 341 (HHR 823) is seen when quite new, in the summer of 1952, at Salisbury bus station, bound for Woodfalls, on the Wiltshire/Hampshire border. Route 44 could still see KSW operation 21 years later (*see Plate 199*). Wilts & Dorset was one of few BTC operators never to employ two or three-line intermediate displays, preferring to show just one name, in large lettering. This picture shows the original position for the bonnet-mounted, white fleet number. Later, the number was placed within a circle, towards the rear of the engine side panel, as shown in *Plate 191*.

*Michael Mogridge*

*Plate 194:* Apart from the destination box modifications, described in *Plate 191*, three other KSWs received modified displays. No. 382 was also fitted with a 'T' box, but Nos. 343 and 386 gained displays of a different kind. Wilts & Dorset was the only BTC operator to change its allegiance from the 'T' box, on new stock, to the alternative side-by-side layout, as seen on the FLF in the background of this photograph. Henceforth, existing vehicles were converted with the side-by-side pattern, including the two KSWs mentioned. The original three-piece equipment was covered by a panel containing the new, centrally-positioned display. After the two KSWs and several LDs had been converted, the company evidently realised that it would be considerably cheaper simply to apply black masking to the glass of the original ultimate site, as shown in *Plates 199 & 200*. No. 343 (HMR 58) is shown racing round the block in the middle of Basingstoke bus station.

*Michael Bennett*

*Plate 195:* Three Wilts & Dorset KSW5Gs were converted to driver trainers. No. 335 (HHR 62) was converted in late 1967, while Nos. 344/58 (HMR 59 and HMR 810) followed in 1971, being renumbered 9092/3 in the Hants & Dorset ancillary vehicle series: No. 335 accordingly became No. 9091. All received enclosed platforms and were adapted as mobile classrooms, in a similar manner to Hants & Dorset's No. 9099 (*see Plate 86 and also Plate 206, for an interior view*). No. 9092 illustrates the yellow livery carried by these three trainers, this particular bus having a Tilling red band between the decks (No. 9093 had a green band, as it was attached to Hants & Dorset's Southampton Depot, although the band was later repainted poppy red). This bus also carries both Wilts & Dorset and Hants & Dorset underlined fleetnames, although subsequently, NBC style Hants & Dorset names were substituted. The oblong registration plate on the radiator was used so that an 'L' plate could be accommodated on the dash. No. 9092 is seen at Winchester in October 1973, ready to depart for its Basingstoke base. It was finally withdrawn in 1976.

*Graham Jones*

*Plate 196:* The first bus of the 1952 order, No. 359 (HMW 445) awaits completion at ECW, in this picture taken in the early summer of 1952. It is still without its seats. The style of the fleetname changed very little over the period from 1946 to 1972, unlike several fellow BTC fleets.

*R. F. Mack*

*Plate 197:* Whilst the 1951 order went mostly to Salisbury, Andover and Amesbury depots, the 1952 buses were allocated predominantly to Basingstoke, for Venture stock replacement. Many stayed throughout their lives and No. 370 (JHR 141) was still allocated there when seen in April 1969, looking extremely well-kept for a 16-year-old vehicle. Wilts & Dorset's buses always looked immaculate, and the black lining-out to the cream bands was maintained until the beginning of the 1970s. Also evident in this view is the rear destination box treatment of No. 343 (HMR 58), which is described in *Plate 194*.

*Graham Jones*

*Plate 198:* In October 1972, the entire Wilts & Dorset stock, including only eighteen KSWs, was transferred to the ownership of Hants & Dorset. By the following April, the only survivors were four KSW5Gs. Then came May 1973, and with it the take-over, by Hants & Dorset, of R. Chisnell's 'King Alfred' services in Winchester. Hants & Dorset needed to inject some extra buses in a hurry, so they relicensed three KSWs there, one of which was No. 371 (HMW 448, which was numbered 362 prior to 1971). This was a 1952 KSW5G, still bearing full Wilts & Dorset livery and fleetnames. The other two were from Hants & Dorset's own fleet and can be seen in *Plate 89*. In this view, King Alfred's statue keeps an eye on this unfamiliar red KSW, waiting at The Broadway on city service 13 to Weeke Estate, in June 1973. (Winchester had witnessed Wilts & Dorset KSWs in earlier days, running in from Basingstoke on service 111). No. 371 was to remain in service until the end of November 1973.

*Graham Jones*

*Plate 199:* Another of the KSW5Gs transferred to Hants & Dorset ownership in October 1972 was No. 381 (JMW 243), formerly numbered 375. Since the early 1970s, regrettably, repaints had not only excluded the black lining to the cream bands, but also eliminated the upper band. Furthermore, as this bus shows, wings were repainted red instead of black, although, tastefully, during 1973, someone restored black to the wings of Winchester's No. 371 (*see Plate 198*). The final detail change to the remaining KSWs, excluding No. 371 again, was the application of NBC-style Hants & Dorset fleet-names, in cream, as illustrated here (Basingstoke's No. 370 differed, by receiving white names, placed centrally). By January 1974, only Nos. 380/1 of the former Wilts & Dorset KSWs remained in service, and subsequently, No. 381, seen here, had the distinction of being the very last low-bridge Bristol double decker in public service within the NBC! It was withdrawn during April 1974. The NBC's only other lowbridge buses after that date were a few Guy Arab IVs with West Riding, and some former Moore Bros., of Kelvedon, 30ft. Guy Arab IVs with Eastern National.

*Allan Macfarlane*

*Plate 200:* Wilts & Dorset's distinctive 1953 batch of fifteen KSW6Bs, with platform doors, were initially allocated to Salisbury and Blandford depots, for use on the company's longest double-deck routes (Blandford operated them on the lengthy service, run jointly with Southern National, to Weymouth). However, as Lodekkas arrived, the batch was redistributed among all depots. No. 392 (KHR 529), the penultimate bus, was, surprisingly, still operating on one of the longest Wilts & Dorset routes, when seen at Newbury bus station as late as June 1970. FS6G No. 639 (677 AAM), seen in the background, beyond Thames Valley's LD6B No. 780 (NBL 737), is the more typical Wilts & Dorset representative of the period.

*Graham Jones*

*Plate 202:* The lower deck of the same bus as shown in *Plate 201* is shown in this view. The KS6B in question is Hants & Dorset No. 1271 (KEL 714), new in September 1950; body No. 4327 on chassis 80.095. The intrusion made by the sunken upper-deck gangway into the lower saloon can plainly be seen, this giving more passengers the need to stoop. Early KS/KSW buses had a circular aperture in the bulkhead, through which the driver and conductor could communicate. Different firms had different ideas about these — some filled them in, others extended the scheme to later KSWs. The seat design was a distinctive feature of the 1950 and 1951 orders. The pattern was derived from a design used by London Transport since before the war, and then installed in 1949/50 Ks and Ls. However, on the KS/KSW seats, the backs were flat, instead of being shaped to provide back support. The foam rubber filling greatly improved comfort over the older seat styles. However, the tops tended to be at shoulder blade level. Moquette, of the famous Tilling 'criss-cross' pattern (red and green on grey), was used up to the 1953 order.

*Phil Davies*

*Plate 203:* With effect from the 1952 order, improved seats were installed, and remained in vogue for the rest of production. Their higher backs made them more comfortable. Polished chrome grab-rails were fitted, contrasting with the satin finish of the earlier frames. The vertical stanchions in this example are non-standard, as it happens, the normal fittings being seen in *Plate 204*. In fact, stanchions were only used in the lower deck of the highbridge buses, lowbridge vehicles having a rail running the length of the sunken gangway moulding. The ECW badge can be seen, applied to the bulkhead. Most operators found there was no need to repaint the white lower saloon ceiling, throughout the entire life of the bus! The vehicle in this photograph is a KSW6G, easy identification being possible due to the bulbous nature of the bell-house casing on the bulkhead. 5LW- and AVW-engined versions had the flat type, as seen in *Plate 202*. Note the revised siting of the cove panel advertisements. The model for this photograph is Hants & Dorset No. 1330 (LRU 59), new in November 1952; body No. 6066 on chassis 94.025.

*Phil Davies*

*Plate 201:* The picture shows what a passenger would see first, on arrival at the top of the stairs of a lowbridge KS. The double-width seats tended to carry only three well-spaced passengers, as a rule, and they would only sit closer together, to admit a fourth person if absolutely necessary! Disembarking from the very inside place of a crowded bus was fraught with difficulty as the roof was so low. The person leaving had to stoop almost double, while also trying to avoid toes, and those remaining had to gather up parcels and bags and to twist their legs out of the way. On cold wet days, the ceiling, just over one's head, could drip condensation down one's neck. Thank goodness for the Lodekka! The unsurpassed excellence of ECW's interior styling resulted in the windows being set flush with the interior panelling, with no fussy ledges or rims. This applied to all bodies from the first 'thin wall' products, as they were termed, on 1949 Ks and Ls, through to the last VRs of 1981. Even the vertical body pillars had half-round cappings. The sunken gangway was not able to reach the front of the bus, as the driver's cab was situated below this point.

*Phil Davies*

*Plate 204:* To the large number of people to whom the lowbridge KSW was the norm, the highbridge version must produce an air of unexpected space, highlighted by the enormous windows and high ceiling. This bus is typical of all 1952-1957 highbridge KSWs. The ECW badge was originally applied above the central front window pillar, but discolouration of the ceiling, due to nicotine, necessitated repainting every four years or so. Until 1953, the fabric used on the seat backs, body walls, etc., was red or green, according to the exterior livery, but from 1954, all buses were trimmed in green. The ribbed aluminium kicking-panel, on the front bulkheads, on both decks, superseded red or green linoleum (*see Plate 202*), and certain operators extended the idea to their earlier buses, notably Bristol. The bus illustrated here, new in August 1954, is Bristol Omnibus Company's No. 8181 (SHW 351), *see Plate 186;* body number 7392 on chassis 102.044.

*Allan Macfarlane*

*Plate 205:* During 1952, West Yorkshire re-equipped one of their lowbridge KSWs with a set of upper-deck seats of their own design. On the new seats, each passenger's place was set back slightly from the one on its left, producing a staggered layout. Reluctance to sit close to other passengers occupying the straight-across bench seat was forcibly overcome with this new design! ECW henceforth adopted the staggered layout as standard from late 1952 order production. The example here is Wilts & Dorset No. 381, which was originally No. 375 (JMW 243), *see Plate 199,* new in June 1953; body No. 5978 on chassis 94.076.

*Allan Macfarlane*

*Plate 206:* Several BTC companies used KSWs for training new drivers, but the extent of the adaption varied widely. Eastern Counties, for example, used a current passenger vehicle, with little more than a removable bulkhead window (*see Plate 62*). On the other hand, Bristol and Hants & Dorset/Wilts & Dorset extensively modified redundant passenger stock, cutting away the offside front bulkhead to enable the instructor to take over the controls in an emergency. Hants & Dorset/Wilts & Dorset made their KSWs into mobile classrooms, by installing a blackboard that could be hinged out of the way. The driver's seat was mounted on a pedestal, instead of the former bulkhead-mounted brackets, the electric switch-box was resited on the body wall, instead of being behind the driver, and a large rear-view mirror was placed on the bulkhead, for the benefit of the instructor, who occupied the forwardmost near-side seat (three pairs of seats, in all, were removed, to ease congestion). The instructor in Bristol's trainers sat on the first offside seat, which was raised to the driver's level, the switch box being positioned in front of the instructor. Whereas Bristol's buses tended to have spare seats removed, especially upstairs, Hants & Dorset/Wilts & Dorset retained them, with additional weights beneath, to simulate a load. Note the addition of the Clayton circular heater in this bus, which is Hants & Dorset/Wilts & Dorset No. 9091 (HHR 62, formerly No. 335), new to Wilts & Dorset in November 1951; body No. 5129 on chassis KSW5G.84.137.

*Allan Macfarlane*

*Plate 207:* The picture reproduced here is, without doubt, the last ever taken of a conventional KSW in regular stage carriage service. The photograph, taken on Saturday, 29th May 1976, shows Bristol Omnibus Company's No. C8374 (WHW 815) at work during the morning, passing along Gloucester Road on route 78. Its companion of the previous few months, No. C8428 (YHT 924), *see Plate 49*, had been laid aside the Monday before and, when this picture was taken, No. C8374 had only a few more hours to live. This bus also illustrates the final condition in which Tilling green KSWs ran for Bristol Omnibus Co. In early 1974, the upper-deck cream band had been painted out, whilst the waistband became white; additionally, the fleetname was moved and amended to the, then, current NBC-style for City buses.

*Gordon Richmond*

*Plate 208:* A large proportion of the KSW family ended their existence in some of the many scrapyards situated in South Yorkshire. However, not all Bristol Omnibus Company buses travelled so far. In fact, of the 22 UHY-registered KSWs with platform doors, Nos. 8265-70 and 8334-49, no fewer than eighteen were broken up by a local scrap dealer, just around the corner from Bristol's central works, in Lawrence Hill — a sad fate indeed for such fine machines (only Nos. 8334-6/42 escaped). There was, however, an ulterior motive behind this move, in that the Gardner 6LW engines were returned to Bristol Omnibus Co. for refitting into FLF6B Lodekkas, during a period when spares for the BVW engine were hard to obtain. The remains of No. 8339 (UHY 387) are seen in July 1972, with an LD6G also in evidence.

*Dave Withers*

*Plate 209:* Since the 1960s, the idea of bus enthusiasts buying redundant or dejected old buses and painstakingly restoring them to their former glory, has grown enormously, so much so that, by the mid-1970s, the diary of events for the summer months would show a gathering or rally for preserved buses every Sunday — at least! Bristol Omnibus Company was not slow to recognise the popularity of such an event when celebrating their centenary in 1974. A rally was held at the British Aerospace car-park in Filton on 9th June, and no fewer than seven KSWs figured amongst the entrants, including some remaining in passenger or driver-training service. At the end of the afternoon, the authors of this book arranged for all seven to be brought together, for a group photograph (many were already parked close to each other). The result is shown here. From the right, the buses, and their owners at that time, were:
UHY 362 Ex-Bristol No. C8322, 1955 KSW6B/H6OR — Phil. Platt, of Exeter; OHY 938 Ex-Bristol No. L8089/W127, 1952 KSW6B/L55RD — Peter Davey, Bristol; NAE 61 Ex-Bristol No. 1801, 1950 KSW6B/H6OR — The authors, Bristol; UHY 360 Ex-Bristol No. C8320, 1955 KSW6B/H6OR — Gordon Bate, Cheshire; UHY 375 Cheltenham District No. 8562, 1955 KSW6G/H6OR — CDTC; UHY 384 Bristol Omnibus Co. No. W143, 1955 KSW6G/H6ORD — Bristol Omnibus Co.; WNO 478 Ex-Eastern National No. 2380, 1953 KSW5G/PO61R — EN Preservation Group.

*Allan Macfarlane*